MW01202068

The Changing

BLUE RIDGE MOUNTAINS

The Changing
BLUE RIDGE MOUNTAINS
ESSAYS ON JOURNEYS PAST & PRESENT

BRENT MARTIN

THE
History
PRESS

Published by The History Press
Charleston, SC
www.historypress.com

Copyright © 2019 by Brent Martin
All rights reserved

Front cover, bottom, photo by Ralph Preston.

First published 2019

Manufactured in the United States

ISBN 9781467142649

Library of Congress Control Number: 2019935355

Notice: The information in this book is true and complete to the best of our knowledge. It is offered without guarantee on the part of the author or The History Press. The author and The History Press disclaim all liability in connection with the use of this book.

All rights reserved. No part of this book may be reproduced or transmitted in any form whatsoever without prior written permission from the publisher except in the case of brief quotations embodied in critical articles and reviews.

If you love the southern Appalachians and Wendell Berry and Annie Dillard and Gary Snyder, read this beautifully written and deeply thought-provoking book.

—Charles Frazier, author of *Cold Mountain*

With unflinching candor, Brent Martin celebrates the heartbreaking beauty of Appalachia. He wrings out every sensory and emotional detail in these passionate, probing essays that explore the wild within. These aren't lyrical paeans to nature; they are gritty, gutsy journeys into the rugged, remote landscapes of the human heart. Immersed in mountain tradition, culture and community, he wanders deep and alone into the wild to find what remains. Martin's powerful, masterful writing shines with real, hard-earned hope.

—Will Harlan, author of the *New York Times* bestseller *Untamed: The Wildest Woman in America*

Brent Martin's essays explore wild spots saved from the wanton disregard of human agency and holy places savored through praise and exquisite literary prose. He reminds me sometimes of Ed Abbey, who before Arches lauded the Smoky Mountains Brent celebrates. But at times Brent's more William Bartram, one of his eco-heroes, striding into the South's great backcountry without a speck of doubt it's still there and it's our job to save it. I plan to give this collection to a few friends who will love it, and mail it to a few assholes who desperately need its salvation, wisdom, and light.

—John Lane, author of *Anthropocene Blues*

With a poet's attention to language and a naturalist's eye for detail, Brent Martin offers us a loving and troubling portrait of the southern Appalachians—the rich history and complexity of the ecosystems alongside the damage that we've wrought on them. Though despair is often on the periphery, he also hears, in the place names of the Cherokee, the writings of William Bartram and the howls and whispers from the wild world, reasons to hope, reasons to hold on.

—Catherine Reid, author of *Falling into Place: An Intimate Geography of Home*

From a man who knows his homeplace well, Brent Martin asks the question "which way is the wilderness?" To answer this question about the future of our natural environment in western North Carolina and the southern Appalachians, he takes us across the landscape to various bioregions and habitats and lets us see for ourselves the beauty and the fragility of these places. His regionally authentic, compassionate and poetic prose raises not only our awareness but our interest in the idea of perpetual preservation. By the end of the book, he most assuredly answers his own question with these words: "Every way. As many ways as can be imagined."

—Thomas Rain Crowe, author of
The End of Eden: Writings of an Environmental Activist

Take a journey. Put aside the common routines of modern life. Step out into the natural world with Brent Martin and strengthen your observation skills, broaden your scientific understanding and pacify your innate, childlike sense of curiosity. Return home on the last page, feeling enlightened, enriched and eager to take your own personal journey of outdoor discovery.

—Marci Spencer, author of *Nantahala National Forest: A History*

Brent Martin is perhaps our most gifted advocate for nature. He writes of wilderness and waterfalls and flowers and fish in prose both clear and passionate. In short, he's both naturalist and poet. Treasure this collection!

—Wayne Caldwell, author of *Cataloochee* and *Requiem by Fire*

A thoughtful and thought-provoking collection of essays from one of Appalachia's staunchest proponents of Wilderness and one of its most devoted writers. Brent Martin is a preeminent naturalist and a scholar of the history of his place. This book is deeply personal, highly instructive, far-reaching.

—Janisse Ray, author of *Ecology of a Cracker Childhood*, among others

CONTENTS

Foreword, by George Ellison   9
Acknowledgements   13

"It's a Good Country; Hold On to It"   15
Snowbird   29
Hunting for Camellias at Horseshoe Bend   43
The Dividing Spring   55
When the Heart Can No Longer Say Home   67
The Sabbatical   75
Fish, Transformation and Thinking Like an Osprey   83
To Know a Tree   89
Three Forks   99
Modern Appalachia and the Death of the Sublime   107
Pushing Through   117
Which Way Is the Wilderness?   125

Index   137
About the Author   143

FOREWORD

How do you discover which book you want to read next? Despite the old adage about not being able to judge a book by its cover, many readers actually do just that by perusing the blurbs on the dust-wrapper. With blurbs, if a favorable one happens to be by an author whose previous books had been enjoyed, that's a good sign. Then there is word of mouth, as well as formal reviews in newspapers, magazines and journals. And finally, there's the "opening paragraph" test, whereby you simply open the book to the first page of text and read the first paragraph to yourself or whoever happens to be listening. If you don't blink your eyes or make a sharp intake of breath or show heightened awareness, why then, that book's probably not your cup of tea. With this test, and almost immediately, you're either on Brent Martin's wavelength or you're not. If so, you're in for a literary roller coaster ride of the sort you can't have anticipated. Even if you can't tell a book by its cover, I agree with novelist-philosopher Walker Percy and many other writers of both fiction and nonfiction that you can tell a lot by its opening paragraph:

> *It is another dark and freezing winter night here in the old Doc Clark home on West Branch, and after several days of rain, I can hear the stream's bold and lonely babble through our bedroom window. It is the season when we are prone to question our decisions and our ability to persevere. The landscape, empty of vegetation, reveals itself in stark shadows and light. I have been reading William Bartram's* Travels *again tonight, focusing on his eighteenth-century description of this area and situating our late nineteenth-century home into that landscape.*

And we are off and running. In the opening paragraphs of the first essay in the collection, Brent is characteristically—especially when alone—in a funk that matches the Thomas Hardy–like weather outside his bedroom window. And like a scene drawn by Hardy, he captures the gloom and doom atmosphere, while at the same time unloosening the strands of his narrative. In the course of a long wintery night, we learn a lot about the inner hopes and ambitions of Brent Martin as he sets out on his quest for a "local habitation" (a place associated with a given community) and a "name" (an identity and a reputation). He is also a poet of some renown in the southern mountains. The descriptive language he employs—especially at the opening or close of an essay—is also remindful of Hardy and other poets he admires, like, say, Emily Dickinson, whose phrase "a Certain slant of Light" (from her "Poem 258") also discombobulates Brent, who no doubt could recite the closing stanza:

> *When it comes, the Landscape listens—*
> *Shadows—hold their breath—*
> *When it goes, 'tis like the Distance*
> *On the look of Death—*

Brent is obsessive about many things. One involves his desire to formulate a sense of place so as to more fully understand who he is. Almost every youngster at one time or another has located himself by scribbling inside the back cover of a schoolbook something like: "Earth, America, North Carolina, Swain County, Bryson City, Toot Hollow, home and me." That sufficed for most. But not for Brent, who casts a somewhat wider net. Lying in his bed looking out his window at the snow that has begun to fall, his mind ranges through space and time from the uplift "that formed these mountains over three hundred million years ago, enormous mountains many thousands of feet higher than they are now, slowly eroding at a pace we are not capable of conceptualizing, our house now sitting where there was once deep soil and stone. Slow, grinding evolution, pathless, and without people for millions and millions of years. I feel that alone."

From that perspective, he moves sure-footedly to the human side of the equation, narrowing his attention to the Cowee valley in present-day Macon County, North Carolina, where he resides. Having noted that "humans have only inhabited Cowee valley for the last ten thousand years or so," he provides a capsule summary of the valley's history. Brent's quests have an action and a name—that is, he yearns to find a place where one might put down roots and establish a worthy reputation. It's a common enough desire but one that in our modern transient and often uprooted world is not so easy to fulfill. And neither are his hopes for environmental awareness and wilderness protection. The following essays both reveal and express these hopes.

—George Ellison

ACKNOWLEDGEMENTS

Several key writer friends over the years have inspired, instructed and guided me in my writing pursuits. One of these, Katherine Stripling Byer, is no longer with us, but her encouragement and her love of Appalachia is an invisible force throughout these scribblings. I'd also like to thank Thomas Rain Crowe, George Ellison, Don Hendershot, John Lane and Janisse Ray for their support over the years. My wife, Angela Faye Martin, has been my closest companion and chief critic throughout all these scribblings. Her creative yet critical eye resides within the entire collection, not to mention her shared passion and artist's love for these great old mountains. My sister Melanie Vickers has been a bulwark in my life, a true friend through thick and thin. Thanks go to the following publications where several of these essays first appeared: *Blue Ridge Outdoors* ("Snowbird," "Three Forks"), *Carolina Mountain Literary Festival Anthology* ("The Sabbatical"), *Earthlines* ("To Know a Tree"), *Kudzu House Quarterly* ("It's a Good Country; Hold On to It," "When the Heart Can No Longer Say Home"), *North Carolina Literary Review* ("Hunting for Camellias at Horseshoe Bend"), *Shanti Arts Quarterly* ("Pushing Through") and *Wildbranch: An Anthology of Nature, Environmental, and Place Based Writing* ("The Dividing Spring").

"IT'S A GOOD COUNTRY; HOLD ON TO IT"

It is another dark and freezing winter night here in the old Doc Clark home on West Branch, and after several days of rain, I can hear the stream's bold and lonely babble through our bedroom window. It is the season when we are prone to question our decisions and our ability to persevere. The landscape, empty of vegetation, reveals itself in stark shadows and light. I have been reading William Bartram's *Travels* again tonight, focusing on his eighteenth-century description of this area and situating our late nineteenth-century home into that landscape.

Bartram passed through our valley less than a mile from our front door, describing Cherokee plantations of corn and beans as he went. Pottery shards and arrowheads found in my garden confirm their presence, and I have often wondered if Doc didn't situate his home on what once had been a Cherokee dwelling. Now I lie in bed and imagine this mountain hollow as it might have appeared 20,000 years ago—an ice age boreal forest of spruce fir, an ecotone resembling something closer to Canada today. I think back further to the geological uplift that formed these mountains over 300 million years ago, enormous mountains many thousands of feet higher than they are now, slowly eroding at a pace we are not capable of conceptualizing, our house now sitting where there was once deep soil and stone. Slow, grinding evolution, pathless and without people for millions and millions of years. I feel that alone.

Humans have only inhabited Cowee valley for the last ten thousand years or so. The first early nomadic bands that arrived here might have arrived

The author's home on a snowy winter day. *Photo by Angela Faye Martin.*

in the hundreds, but we will never know. They likely prospered, and there is evidence of settled agriculture that dates back four thousand years to support this. The Native American mound building culture that developed sometime around the ninth century AD was largely wiped out by diseases introduced by Spanish explorers in the sixteenth century. The Cherokees who followed them created a vibrant town in Cowee that did well until the French and Indian War of the 1760s. There was another wave of destruction of Cowee during the American Revolution, but the Cherokees hung on here until their Jacksonian-era removal in 1838. American settlers hungry for land followed, and then the Civil War, followed by industrialist timber interests, world wars and their attendant worker Diasporas and now this.

The road outside is glazing over with ice. Tomorrow, it will be covered with snow. We will likely be here for a few days before venturing out. We will be without power soon, but we are prepared. There is firewood stacked on the porch for the wood stove, batteries for the CD player, propane for our camp stove and plenty of candles. It will be silent, and we will write. And I don't really mind the not venturing out. I will be forced to be bored, and I can use it. If there is one thing we twenty-first-century Americans could use a good dose of, it is some forced and productive boredom.

A hundred years ago, the road outside stopped at our house. There was nothing above us but the towering Cowee range, likely stripped of timber at that time, with cattle grazing and corn growing on the rugged hillsides. Today, it goes for another mile before turning back at the edge of the national forest and heading down the mountainside opposite us. Empty second homes dot its path in winter, many of them likely in bank ownership after the last real estate collapse. One of the Clark daughters who is in her nineties stops by every once in a while with her daughter, who always drives up out front, rolls down the window and yells, "Mama says she wanted to go home." Upon her first visit here, the elderly woman stood outside the car, looked up at the mountains above us, swept her hands about and said, "My daddy sold all that land to the government for a dollar an acre."

Yes, he did, and the government agency, the U.S. Forest Service, eventually purchased almost half the county. This, in turn, led to the area becoming a major recreation and second-home destination, with almost half the county's property tax bills now being sent out of state. Cowee, once the vibrant diplomatic capital of the Middle Town Cherokees, followed by agricultural American Cowee, is now a mishmash of retired Floridians, second-home owners, "locals" and those who have moved here for "quality of life" reasons—a broad spectrum of back-to-the-landers, post-suburban dropouts, survivalists, fundamentalists and New Age eschatologists.

IT IS AN EXCEPTIONALLY warm July morning, soon to be very hot, and I am standing on top of the Cowee mound, the once ceremonial center and diplomatic capital of the Middle Town Cherokees. In my hand is the *Harper's* edition of William Bartram's *Travels*, hefty and covered in sweat after the march here from the end of the gravel road by the Little Tennessee River. There are perhaps twenty-five people around me, and they are waiting for me to read Bartram's description of the mound and the council house that once stood here. I am amazed that so many people turn out on a weekday in this remote location to hear and talk about one of America's first and most well-known naturalists. Bartram passed through here in May 1775 on his journey to the Cherokee Overhill Towns near present-day Loudon, Tennessee, but he stopped in Cowee for an extended visit, exploring the area while waiting on a guide.

This is the heart of the southern Blue Ridge; look in any direction from here and there are mountains. To the west, the Nantahala range runs roughly north, paralleling the river and eventually reaching a dead end at the Great Smoky Mountains National Park. To the east, the Cowee range looms closer, with Cowee Bald, a sacred mountain to the Cherokees, standing out starkly among the ridgeline's many peaks. Studded with radio and cell towers, it is not hard to locate. To the north, the Unaka range of the Great Smokies is a distant hazy blue, barely discernible. It is apparent to all here why Bartram described Cowee as one of the most charming mountain landscapes perhaps anywhere to be seen. This event has been advertised as an outing to learn more about Bartram and his time in the Little Tennessee Valley, and since this rural area has a large retirement and second-home population, I suppose I shouldn't be surprised at such a large weekday turnout. If you have lived here long, you have likely heard his name.

Cowee mound, the once diplomatic center of the Middle Town Cherokees. *Photo by Ralph Preston.*

Bartram's path to Cowee in 1775 began in Charleston, South Carolina, from which he traveled up through Keowee, the principal town of the Lower Town Cherokees in northwest South Carolina, and across to the headwaters of the Little Tennessee near present-day Mountain City, Georgia. From there, he turned north and followed the river as it wound through a landscape largely empty of humans, passing through the empty Cherokee village of Nikwasee, a spiritual center yet to recover from the damage inflicted upon it during the French and Indian War. Today, the mound is a tiny green island surrounded by the town of Franklin, where such reverential honorifics as Indian Mound Realty, Hot Spot Convenience Store and Black Dog Guns spill forth from the mound's tenuous base.

His description of "the great Vale of Cowee" is replete with the language of someone at once in love with the natural beauty of the world yet struggling with its harshness and the plight of its inhabitants—not to mention his own internal drama. The passages are filled with luminous descriptions of the plant world, Cherokee customs and characteristics, the violent and destructive forces of Appalachian weather and what my friend Brad Sanders has referred to in his *Guide to William Bartram's Travels* as the "Southern Paradise Lost." I have always considered *Travels* a bittersweet and melancholic interpretation of the eighteenth-century southern landscape, a landscape on the great verge of something, and a reading never leaves me without feeling a bit wistful, even nostalgic for what is likely an over-romanticized past.

I think of Bartram as America's first hippie and one of the only eighteenth-century Americans who still has groupies. The Seminoles named him Puc Puggy, or, in English, the Flower Seeker. He was a Quaker pacifist at odds with his father, longing for his respect. There are annual conferences, biographies, anthologies, epic poems and trail societies that exalt his legacy. I've dressed as Bartram and taken groups down the Little Tennessee River in canoes to hear about him and to experience this view from the mound. I've looked for his original route up the Cowee mountains with historical map expert Lamar Marshall, read my own poems about him out loud, read his *Travels* to groups while dressed as I thought he might have dressed and spent one long winter slowly reading Philip Lee Williams's four-hundred-page epic poem *The Flower Seeker*, each line going down in me like a sip of old smoky bourbon. It might best be described as an affliction.

Bartram's language for this landscape is rich with the adjectives of respect and awe, and I find myself going back to passages of his in order to ground myself here in a way that makes me view my homeplace geography with

The Nantahala Mountains, described by Bartram as the "Jore" mountains. *Photo by Ralph Preston.*

hope. His visit to Cowee on the eve of the American Revolution was over a decade after the French and Indian War, and the landscape had been stripped of the Cherokees' original glory and magnificence. Like most Anglo explorers and military adventurists of his day, he found the place intimidating, though his is the only account that expresses such intimidation simultaneously with rapture and awe. His description of the view west from the Nantahala Mountains is a powerful expression of this: "I began to ascend the Jore Mountains, which I at length accomplished, and rested on the most elevated peak, from whence I beheld with rapture and astonishment, a sublimely awful scene of power and magnificence, a world of mountains piled upon mountains."

Not long after his descent into the Nantahala River drainage, Bartram retreated from his original plan to reach the Cherokee Overhill Towns and returned to Cowee. It wasn't just the lonely and intimidating landscape before him; he had encountered on his path Atakullahkullah, the well-known and respected Cherokee chief, who gave him a friendly warning of colonial troubles in the Overhill Towns.

I believe he also heard a lonesome note within these mountains and hollows, including one that exudes that certain melancholy that Emily Dickinson tapped into with her certain slant of light. I have experienced this in the mountains of Appalachia my entire life. I think that the spirit world here runs deep, an expression of the hundreds of millions of years of the birth, death and decay of an unparalleled world of plant and animal life. Walk the rich coves of Appalachia on an early spring morning and you will not deny the power of this dark and evocative bouquet. Thomas P. Slaughter, in *The Natures of John and William Bartram*, has written about Bartram's suffering of melancholia. Among the letters that Slaughter uses to support this is one of southern planter Henry Laurens, whose description of Bartram's condition upon his visit to Bartram's backwoods struggling Florida farm suggests suicidal tendencies. Laurens's letter to William's father states matter-of-factly that "William simply wasn't fit for the world in which other men lived."

Bartram did compare himself to Nebuchadnezzar while traveling in the Nantahala Mountains, expelled from the society of men and constrained to roam in the mountains and wilderness, there to herd and feed with the wild beasts of the forest. He describes his journey into the mountains of Cowee as a "lonesome pilgrimage" and speaks of the "dreary mountains." More than once, he describes the landscape sinking his spirits. I ask Brad Sanders what he thinks about Slaughters's assertion, as well as my own feelings about the Appalachians having their own unnerving certain slant of light.

To the first question, Brad tells me:

> *I am not so sure that Bartram was melancholy, but maybe just introverted and introspective. His* bête noire *was that he had to live and work in a society that required him to behave differently, mainly work for a living at a career that he did not like just so he could have money. He was by no means a recluse, because everybody he met found him to be charming and interesting. He must have had a gift for conversation and diplomacy. One thing that is telling is that he was friends with Alexander Cameron and George Galphin, who despised one another even while each admired and aided Bartram. Bartram was able to move in many circles of society and was able to befriend most people he met. This may have a lot to do with his introspection—he didn't place demands on people, and neither did he approach them with any preconceived ideas. Late in life, he was content to live under his brother's roof and tend the garden for subsistence. He needed something more than a career; he needed his vocation to be the meaning of his life, and that was a hard thing to do, then as now. Could Bartram's failure to marry have as much to do with his not wanting to take on that kind of responsibility, meaning a legitimate career, as it did with his introversion?*

As for my own feelings about the lonesomeness of the place, Brad says:

> *As Bartram traveled across the Nantahalas and got deeper into the mountains and farther from white civilization, he began to lose his nerve and turned back. Was it because he was afraid of being ambushed, or was it because the landscape was so dark and foreboding, even for William Bartram? I do see the Appalachians as more dark, personal and secretive than the Sierra Nevadas and Rocky Mountains, which are much grander and more open. There is something much more foreboding about the darkness, softness and solitude of the Appalachians.*

I ask Jim Kautz the same question. Jim is author of *In the Footsteps of William Bartram*, a modern-day palimpsest of Bartram's path around the Southeast. Kautz now lives in Cowee, where he and his wife, Maria, live in a house perched on a small knoll overlooking Bartram's path, approximately a mile from the old town's center. He is with us today at the mound.

> *Slaughter was, in my opinion, overreaching. I think it is a vain quest to diagnose someone 230 years later, especially when we have few sources and our main source [*Travels*] was published almost 20 years after his experience (they are not contemporaneous). That said, I observe that Bartram reported lively experiences with other people. He delights in food, dances and even a gigantic snake when in the presence of others. His blue moments are always when he is alone. Perhaps his depressed state in the Nantahala mountains has less to do with "nature" than with his statement, "After waiting two days at Cowe expecting a guide and protector to the Overhill towns, and at last being disappointed, I resolved to pursue the journey alone, though against the advice of the traders; the Overhill Indians being in an ill humour with the whites, in consequence of some late skirmishes between them and the frontier Virginians, most of the Overhill traders having left the nation."*

AFTER READING BARTRAM'S DESCRIPTION of the Cherokee council house and the evening's festivities that he witnessed on this very spot, we descend the mound and fan out as we wander down to the river's edge. There is a large assemblage of mortar stones in the river that were used for unknown years by Native Americans. Some of these rocks are six feet across, pockmarked with smooth depressions used for grinding. We stand at the river's edge and stare down at the stones. The bank is now a good eight feet above the river here, the result of years of poor modern agricultural practices and deforestation of the stream bank. At some distant date, the river would have joined the bank in a more agreeable fashion, and this deeply cut eroding bank is a stark example of the negative impacts from the valley's current inhabitants.

There is a thin line of honey locusts along the river's edge, a species known for its sweet pulp-filled pods that is native to regions west of here. They were introduced here by the Cherokees and became so prolific in

Cullasaja
Falls on the
Cullasaja River.
*Photo by Ralph
Preston.*

the valley that there are place names that can be traced to them. Cullasaja means "sugar place" in Cherokee, and given that the Cullasaja River is one of the main tributaries of the Little Tennessee, it must have been a major location for collecting these long brown pods. There are other species that were introduced here by the Cherokees for their food and medicinal values, species like yaupon holly (*Ilex vomitoria*), native to the coastal plain and widely used by southeastern Indians as a ceremonial emetic. Bartram described the species' presence here in 1775, and though many have looked for it in recent years, it has believed to have vanished with the Cherokee towns that sustained it.

All about the mound are specimens of *Passiflora incarnata*, or maypops as I called them as a child. The tart fruits from this plant are high in vitamin C, and they, too, were cultivated for food, drink and medicinal purposes by the Cherokees. There is also *Yucca filamentosa*, another southeastern native, but cultivated here for its utility, along with a wide variety of other native grasses. River cane (*Arundinaria gigantea*) is also returning and is abundant in places along the river—ethnobotanical artifacts all, and their presence here a constant reminder of the valley's rich cultural past. The Cherokees use river cane to this day for baskets, blowguns, arrows and likely many other things, but Bartram does not include it in his long inventory of plant and tree species that he encountered while traveling through the area.

Another mystery is his omission of Red Spruce. Most of the authorities on Bartram's route believe that he traveled up the Cowee Range along Huckleberry Branch and that his much-discussed encounter with Cherokee maidens picking strawberries was at what locals call "Alarka Laurel." Alarka Laurel is the southernmost reach of Red Spruce and is a stark anomaly among the Cowee Mountains' dominant oak-hickory forests. It is a relic forest from the last ice age and is a harbor of numerous rare species more common in northern zones. Yet there is no mention of it in Bartram's inventory, and one is left to surmise that he was so distracted by this "sylvan scene of primitive innocence" and his admission that it was perhaps "too enticing for hearty young men" that he simply forgot to pay it mention, though this would be hard to believe.

Regardless, to live here today in Cowee is to live among the ghosts of previous inhabitants and the abundant relics of their civilization. The mound lies within the heart of the Cowee National Historic District, and at 370 acres, it is the largest in western North Carolina. Within a seven-mile reach of the Little Tennessee River as it flows through Cowee are thirteen Native American fish weirs. The weirs are constructed of stone and are

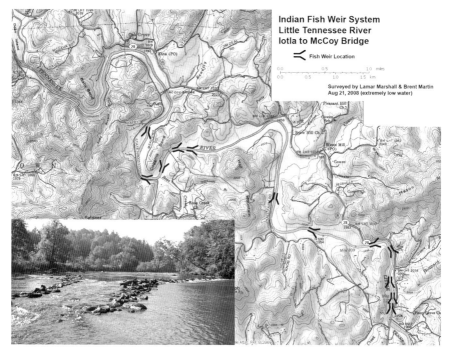

Native American fish weirs on a seven-mile stretch of the Little Tennessee River near Cowee. *Mapwork by Lamar Marshall.*

V-shaped, large and hidden in many places from centuries of sedimentation and weather that have left them discernible only during times of drought. I spent one hot summer afternoon dragging a canoe through this seven-mile stretch with Lamar Marshall, poling along carefully as he mapped each one and assigned it a GPS point.

Fish biologist Dr. William Mclarney tells me that the weirs were likely used to capture redhorse, a large carp-like fish that once populated the Little Tennessee in great numbers before impoundments limited their spawning migrations. It is not a far stretch of the imagination to envision a glorious summer day in Cowee as Cherokees gathered in great numbers to run the fish downstream into these structures, where they were captured in large wicker baskets as they were funneled through the V's narrow open end. Today, their numbers greatly reduced, they nonetheless travel the river in thick amber schools, easily spooked as I fish the shoals, but with no local culture to face down each year as their once abundant ancestors did.

The vegetation along the river is thick. We push through blackberry brambles, dense river cane and a tangle of invasive exotics—Japanese honeysuckle, multiflora rose, privet, Oriental bittersweet and more. A local wild foods expert is extolling the virtue of many of these species and doggedly argues with us as we curse our way through. She tells us we must stop our eradication campaigns and instead learn to live and work with them. It's a tough crowd, and no one agrees. Later, she gives me the book *Invasive Plant Medicine: The Ecological Benefits and Healing Abilities of Invasives* in hopes of persuading me, but I'm not there yet. I have lived among these species long enough to know that if I left for one growing season, my garden and home would likely disappear under them. Bartram would not approve.

We push on, we humans, the most destructive and invasive of species, and emerge on the old gravel road that was once the main route to Cowee town and the mound. Today, the main route through Cowee is a mile away on the opposite side of the river, a paved two-lane known as State Highway 28. Loud Harleys are roaring up the valley, a grim augur's din that grows each year like the privet, a sound that signifies some strange need to dominate, to be seen, to be heard in a world where sounds grow and drown and silence is something to escape.

As we are departing, a few of us agree to eat lunch at the Cowee Convenience Store. It is the only store in Cowee, a modern little place with a deli, picnic tables, cheap action film DVDs and an assortment of camo hats and Rebel flag paraphernalia. True to its Cowee roots, it also serves as an ersatz council house where retired local residents gather in pasty clumps to drink coffee and muse the local affairs. There is a pack of motorcyclists refueling before they continue on their way north, as it is the last outpost for twenty miles. From here they will turn north and scream down the still wild Little Tennessee River until they reach its impoundment at Lake Fontana, where they will turn up the path Bartram would have taken had he continued on his way to the Overhill Towns. Their departure is deafening.

THERE IS DEEP SILENCE in the Cowee winter night, and snow is falling without our knowing. In a thousand years, will anyone lie here on such a night conjuring up this place and its past inhabitants? But for the wildlife and wind, and those whose restlessness calls them forth, the land will be still for a little while, a rare reprieve for this ancient trodden-upon ground. The gas generators will crank, the snow plows will arrive and my neighbor and his tractor with the dozer blade will soon be out scraping our gravel road. No one knows how to stay home anymore. When the screens go silent, it is a call to action.

Though most of the current inhabitants love this valley, we are leaving a deep imprint upon it with our roads and ridgetop homes, burrowing on with our high-impact lifestyles and commodity-driven addictions. And like most rural communities within proximity of major urban centers, our edges are being pressed by boondoggle DOT road projects and mega developments like the Super Walmart being built just ten miles to the north of us. We are being pursued by Anywhere America, a homogenized landscape void of character and substance. Yet Cowee is still the most charming landscape perhaps anywhere to be seen, with its large assemblage of protected public and private lands. Nineteenth-century ethnographer James Mooney describes an event that was told to him by James Watford that is worth telling. Watford was a mixed blood who lived among the Cherokees and was raised in the Valleytown near modern-day Andrews, North Carolina. In 1891, Mooney considered him the last living link to the area's Cherokee past and traditions. Watford told Mooney of an incident when Cowee Cherokees encountered a Shawnee prisoner who had escaped Cowee and had later returned during more peaceful times on a hunting trip. As Watford described it, the Shawnee stood on an opposing hill and called out to them, "Do you still own Cowee?" When they answered that they did, the Shawnee, who encouraged them not to sell any more lands, said, "Well, it's the best town of the Cherokee. It's a good country; hold on to it.'

The Cherokees now own the Cowee mound and the sixty acres that surround it, and there is an ongoing effort to conserve the remaining farmland and working forests that lie within its historic realm. To see the return of this mound to them in my lifetime, and to be there at the occasion, was something I will not forget. That is perhaps the most hopeful aspect of living here—the concentration of conscientious objectors, a modern-day cadre of Bartrams who are working to conserve the place and its traditions.

I rise, light the woodstove and watch the snow fall for a while until the coffee is ready. The world outside is gray, black and white. Crows are coming up the hollow as they always do, and I watch and admire their great melodramatic energy. Such a harsh, cold, lovely morning, and yet they rise to the occasion as they always do, with tremendous pluck and commitment. It is a good country, I think, the best of what is left in this shrinking rural landscape. And we will work to hold on to it.

SNOWBIRD

Wilderness. The word itself is music. Wilderness, wilderness…we scarcely know what we mean by the term, though the sound of it draws all whose nerves and emotions have not yet been irreparably stunned, deadened, numbed by the caterwauling of commerce, the sweating scramble for profit and domination.
—Edward Abbey

There is a storm brewing along the spine of the Snowbird Mountains. Dark purple skies are rolling about us here at five thousand feet on the Cherohala Skyway, where our small car sits dwarfed within vast mountains in the Hooper Bald parking lot. We are packing up the last of our items for a three-day trip into the headwaters of Big Snowbird Creek and are trusting the forecast that the skies will soon clear and allow us a couple of nights of peace and isolation in this nine-thousand-acre chunk of wildness known as the Snowbird Wilderness Study Area. A loud Harley pulls up as we are closing our packs, and two chunky and leather-clad passengers hop off, smiling and asking about our trip. They are both from south Georgia, accent proven, and have not been on the Skyway before. Like most people who travel its path for the first time, they cannot believe the beauty and the miles of unbroken wild and forested landscape.

While my wife, Angela, visits the Forest Service restrooms, I read the interpretive sign that borders the trail leading to the top of nearby Hooper Bald. There was once a hunter resort at this spot, built in 1908 by George Moore, who transported elk, grizzlies, Russian boar, mule deer and wild turkeys here before tiring of the project and giving the lodge to Garland "Cotton" McGuire, who lived here until the 1940s. A large-caliber bullet hole resides in the center of the hard plexiglass, and all of the trailhead signs have been torn off their posts. As we walk away from the car, I realize we could likely return to broken windows and flat tires. I tell Angela that one of my predecessors in my current job as regional director for the Wilderness Society was reportedly burned in effigy during the last Wilderness wars here in 1984.

Graham County, North Carolina, is 80 percent federally owned and is flanked on its western sides by one of the largest concentrations of roadless land in the East. Joyce Kilmer–Slickrock Wilderness lies just to our north, and the Citico Wilderness lies directly to our west. And to the north of all of this is the half-million-acre Great Smoky Mountains National Park. Snowbird was designated a Wilderness Study Area by Congress in 1984, when North Carolina had its last Wilderness legislation. The Forest Service did not agree with Congress, and as it did not recommend the area for Wilderness in its last management plan revision, it has remained in a state of limbo—the Forest Service cannot cut it or build roads into it, but it has no lasting protection either. Multiple bills in Congress at this moment would strip it and others like it of this type of destination.

We walk the manicured tourist trail that is a short walk to the top of Hooper Bald, searching as we go for the Kings Meadow trailhead, our path down to the headwaters of Big Snowbird Creek. When we find what we think is the trail, the sign for it has been ripped or shot off its post. The trail is faint, and we pick our way down over fallen birches, losing the trail occasionally and unsure we are even on it until we at last come to a crossroads where a sign survives, only due to its inaccessibility. Here we at last get onto the Mitchell Lick Trail, the old wagon road that Moore brought his wild game in on, which appears to be rarely used by hikers, though showing signs of illegal off-road vehicle (ORV) use. Along the way, we cross a high-elevation stream where at some point there was likely an Indian hunting camp. Worked quartz flakes lie about in clusters, and I pocket several for souvenirs from our trip.

It is late April, and the neo-tropical migrants are arriving. Anxious about finding the side trail down to Big Snowbird Creek, I try to hide my anxiety from Angela by identifying them and the many spring ephemeral plants that dot the rich slopes. Black-throated blue warbler, black-throated green warbler, Parula, black and white warbler, ovenbird. Ramps, Canada mayflower, trailing arbutus, broad beech fern. I say these words out loud, and they roll off my tongue in search of spirit. *Look at the stunning bronze buds of these beech trees, Angela. Everything is fine.* Knowing me all too well, she confronts me on the way down and asks me when I'm going to relax. I tell her that as soon I know where I am and know where we are sleeping I will.

Eventually, we see an overgrown path that could be our passage down to Big Snowbird Creek, though it is nothing more than a faint break in the forest floor marked with old plastic blue flagging. I'm fine for a while, pushing through and thinking this has got to be it, but then begin to think that it could be directions to a meth lab or pot field. As little use as this area gets, I would not be surprised at all. I'm again filled with a crazed anxiety— that Angela picks up on—and I keep this one explanation of it all to myself. Angela has been the victim of a violent crime, and one of my worst fears is of her having to face another. When the perpetrator was released from prison after twenty-one years, I slept with a loaded .38 in the drawer next to me for almost two years. I don't worry about wild animals out here; I worry about wild people. The more we enter this wild place, the more I relax though. People for the most part stay near roads, and given the overall health rating of most Americans, the farther I am from a road the better I feel.

We at last make it to Big Snowbird Creek and find the designated Big Snowbird Creek Trail. There is little left of it, but a few yellow birches are blazed with blue paint. The trail has seen such little use in recent years that we lose it completely at times between blazes. At one point, I hear a broad winged hawk above us, and at the moment I tell Angela, I trip and fall hard onto the rocky and indiscernible trail. It is not easy to rise from, but trying to keep the spirit of our retreat alive, I tell Angela that I should have never said, "Broad winged hawk!" For the rest of the trip, whenever she sees or hears what is likely the same hawk, she pronounces it excitedly and then fakes a fall. My ankle is screaming, but I'm supposed to think it's funny.

Occasionally, we cross old chestnut railroad trestles from the logging days, moss covered, protruding from rich black ooze. Bemis Lumber bought all of the Big Snowbird drainage in 1924 and laid waste to the timber. It did leave these old and gnarly yellow birches up here in the high country, their progeny now filling the forest floor about them in a great spectrum of age classes. There are also a few large buckeyes and striped maple, but the tree diversity is likely a fraction of what it was when Bemis logged the area. The young birches are golden and their bark peels back in large smooth flakes that we attempt to write and draw upon.

There are no flat spots for camping, but after the third crossing of Big Snowbird, we see a place back in the rhododendron that appears to have been a campsite at some distant time. The fire ring stones are almost

Big Snowbird Creek, Snowbird Wilderness Study Area. *Photo by Brent Martin.*

unidentifiable under a thick bed of leaves and debris, but there is an almost flat spot for a tent, and it is at least fifty feet back off the trail, hidden. Several piles of fresh coyote scat mark the trail at this point, and our dog, Izzy, looks about nervously as we put up the tent and clear out a place for cooking. The fugitive Eric Rudolph claims to have hid out in Graham County for a while, and this would seem as likely a spot as any. No one seems to have been here in years.

A deep loneliness permeates this place. I feel it, and Angela does as well. I'm sure some of it has to do with the remoteness and lack of human presence, but something else calls as well. I have always felt an intrinsic melancholy in these mountains, something that is perhaps the result of hundreds of millions of years of birth, death and decay. This was the last part of western North Carolina to be descended upon by white settlers and is the place to which the Cherokee leader Tsali and his fellow resistors to removal fled during the Trail of Tears. The descendants of these resistors now make up the Snowbird Cherokee community that borders the eastern boundary of the Wilderness Study Area.

As we are preparing supper, I open up a box of Bandit Brand Merlot that has "Ten Good Reasons to Buy Wine in a Box" broadcast on its side. Among my favorites: #3: Lower Shipping Weight = Less Fuel Emissions; #7: One Truckload of Empty Bandit Boxes = 26 Truckloads of Glass Wine Bottles; #10: You Can Crush It on Your Forehead When Done. We finish the wine after a dinner of Seeds of Change Organic Dharmsala Aromatic Indian Rice Blend and Jyoti Mung Dahl (yes, that is really what we had), along with some wild ramps I pick on the way down, but we have no inclination to smash the box into our foreheads, even after a couple of shots of good Clay County moonshine. Tired, full and a little drunk, we turn in early, but neither of us can sleep.

Izzy squirms about at the end of the tent, dreaming of coyotes, and I lie and talk to Angela about jobs, music (her profession), dreams and lost dreams and the work required to permanently protect a place like this. I'm fifty-two and tired of fighting, but still the word calls me on. Wilderness. The word has been so divisive that I sometimes think we need a new word to replace it. Why not? The Cherokees had no word for it, so couldn't I, too, learn to treat the whole planet as wildness once and now wildness lost? Forget the categories? Yet the word itself has power and still fires my imagination. In *Wilderness and the American Mind* (1967), author and historian Roderick Nash presented modern Anglo-Americans with their history and relationship to the word, dating back to early Teutonic and

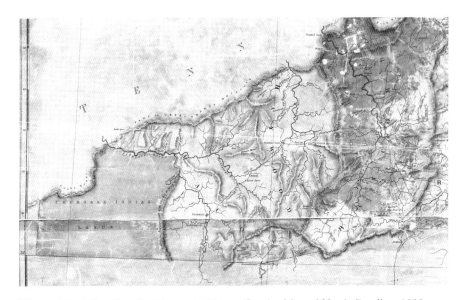

Western North Carolina detail from the Macrae-Brazier Map of North Carolina, 1833. *Courtesy of Library of Congress.*

Norse languages. Its origin and earliest usage seem to imply the word's meaning as being self-willed or uncontrollable, conveying the idea of lost, disordered or confused. Old English *deor* was prefixed with *wild* to denote wild creatures not under the control of man, and the earliest usage of *wildeor* was in the eighth-century epic *Beowulf*, which referred to savage animals inhabiting desolate regions of forests, crags and cliffs.

By the seventeenth century, the word was anathema to everything civilized. Puritan ministers arriving in the New World railed against the howling Wilderness that had to be conquered in the name of Christianity. The pastoral ideal was dominant, and Wilderness was what stood in the way of it. Yet as the woods were felled and the natives conquered, the religious idea of Deism and the scientific era known as the Enlightenment were gaining strength. Deism sought to merge God and nature as one, while the Enlightenment sought to explain natural phenomena in divine yet rational terms. Wilderness got a new lease on life with these two movements, with the first American to advance such notions being the eighteenth-century naturalist William Bartram, who has been credited with being the first American to romanticize and elevate the American landscape to the sublime. Over the next 150 years, the literary and artistic movement known as Romanticism further elevated wild nature as representative of simplicity, freedom and religious bliss. Yet the Romantics, coming from more urbane, literary and educated backgrounds, remained at odds with frontier Americans, who took great pride in subjugating Wilderness and transforming it into civilization. This divide continues in many ways unto this day, as rural Americans stereotype environmentalists as naïve city dwellers who know nothing of working and living off the land, while environmentalists stereotype Wilderness opponents as insensitive, selfish and ignorant of the impacts they are making on places that environmentalists are trying to protect.

Yet I don't believe early Wilderness advocates can be characterized this way. Though many of their ideas can be tied directly to the Romantic movement, early conservationists such as Aldo Leopold saw the landscape in its entirety and sought to understand the interdependency of all living things. Farming and logging could be done in a way to preserve the long-term health of the land (of which he did both), while arguing that Wilderness could serve as a baseline for learning how the parts all worked together when protected from the heavy and manipulative hand of modern humans.

The word today has become so politicized and culturally laden, attacked by hunters, fishermen, mountain bikers, trail clubs, off-road vehicle riders and the very agencies that are supposed to support it, that to be an advocate for it is to place yourself on the margins and at odds with most user groups. It's an idea that people seem to have fallen out of love with after almost fifty years of its codification into law with the 1964 Wilderness Act. Yet run a Google image search of the word "wilderness" and you will see that we use it as a marketing tool for just about any type of consumer product, everything from mustard to off-road vehicles, dog food, soap and deodorant. It's part of the American identity, yet we don't seem to want any more of it, and what we do have is highly suspect among many interests.

Angela tells me that she had no idea that this was such a beautiful place, though I have told her about it for several years. We could move to Stecoah, she says, and then we could be close by and have much better chances for success in protecting it. Stecoah is in Graham County and considerably more forward thinking, but, I tell her, it is still in Graham County. As the last dry county in western North Carolina, I tell her, we'd be driving thirty miles for a six-pack of beer. And it's a place with a reputation. The writer Peter Jenkins spent a harrowing week trapped here while walking and working his way across America and chronicled it in his 1977 book *A Walk Across America*. Most Americans would be familiar with the location unknowingly, having seen the movie *Nell*, which was filmed nearby, or seeing Harrison Ford rappel down the nearby Cheoah dam for the movie *The Fugitive*. Or they might have seen one of the Discovery Channel's recent episodes of *Moonshiners*, in which Graham County figures prominently.

After a fitful night's sleep of strange dreams of falling buildings and distorted faces of the past, I wake to the psychedelic babblings of a winter wren. At the nearby point where we left the trail to make camp here there are two fresh piles of coyote scat, marking their territory. I respond in kind and hope that they will respect our little camp for a few days and give Izzy a wide berth. My neighbors shoot them for sport and out of multiple beliefs, such as the coyotes are out to kill their lap dogs and house cats, are destroying wild game populations and will soon take over the planet and implement a socialist dictatorship. The day before arriving here, we sat in a Waynesville tavern over beers and supper watching a cable television show where two beefy, red-faced hunters showed their skills enticing coyotes into an open field with fake rabbits. The ORVs they rode in on were enormous, piled with rifles and gear needed to make a hunter's blind and other accoutrements. The machismo behind it all was unnerving. I thought they would probably be more than happy to use me as such a decoy for my beliefs and love of coyotes.

After a breakfast of summer sausage, Havarti cheese and sliced apples, we head downstream for exploration. Painted trillium is blooming and abundant, and bluets line the faded path we wander along, listening to the neo-tropicals sing. Not far downstream below our campsite we stop for a while to wander within a rich hillside of spring ephemerals. We wander on a bit, crossing Big Snowbird three dry times, hopping rocks and logs, before the fourth downstream crossing, where Angela loses interest out of fear of falling into the growing and increasingly deep water. It is luxurious and unnatural to move this slow and without destiny—an adjustment for us as we detach our lives from the demands of gadgets.

So much green is emerging in the grays and dark browns. Bryophyte-carpeted boulders protrude from the stream's rugged banks. Just downstream, some large buckeyes congregate around the broken trunk of an enormous yellow birch, along with some sections of old railroad track, half covered in decades of leaf mold and decay. Rotting but intact chestnut trestles still rise from the soft, watery earth.

Back at the tent for lunch, we talk about the frenetic nature of our rural lives. People we know in cities think we live some idyllic existence out here—and often they are right—but it's far from being a cakewalk. I'm beating the old dead horse again with my weariness of working to protect places such as these—the tiresome polarization, opposition and misinformation that must constantly be dealt with and the incredible energy and resources needed to get a bill passed—and Angela speaks to me of the weariness of attempting to be an artist and musician in a world that is cheapened and dumbed down daily by electronic "social networking." Though protecting wild places has never been without some controversy, it wasn't always as divisive as it is now. When Congress passed the Wilderness Act in 1964, it passed the House and Senate unanimously. It took eight years, and countless revisions and compromises, but the bipartisan bill passed unanimously— an unimaginable legislative scenario here in the early twenty-first century.

What went wrong with Wilderness? What has changed since 1964 that has made permanently protecting a fraction of our public lands from resource extraction, road building and mechanized recreation and equipment such a controversial action? One shift has been that since 1964, our oil addiction as a nation has been expanded to weed-eaters, chain saws and other mechanical means of lawn maintenance and woods work. Trail clubs, which supported and were critical to the Wilderness Act's passage in 1964, have become dependent on these tools to care for trails, and the problem is compounded with a volunteer-based aging membership and the lack of youth recruitment and interest. Opposition to Wilderness from trail clubs has been the hardest pill to swallow.

Other trail user groups have emerged since the act's passage. Mountain bikes, nonexistent in 1964, are now as common in the national forest as the dark-eyed juncos flitting about our camp. Now one of the most highly organized recreational uses in the nation, many bikers have a hard time accepting that they aren't allowed in Wilderness, and many of them do not support any new designations and would like to have the act revised to allow them. The relatively cheap off-road vehicles commonly known as four wheelers had yet to be developed in 1964, so the highly organized opposition they muster on Wilderness designations today did not exist then.

A large percentage of hunters feel that Wilderness limits the type of management they believe will produce more game and want more cutting of the forest in order to increase the numbers of species they believe want the young forage and cover produced by cutting, such as deer and ruffed grouse. Crafters of the Wilderness Act made sure to impose no limits on hunting, and large sportsmen organizations were strong supporters of the act's passage. Yet state game agencies that manage much of the land that surrounds Wilderness have made a strong and convincing case to hunters

"Welcome to the Fabulous Anthropocene Era." *By artist Robyn Woolston.*

that Wilderness limits their management options, thereby leading to a decrease in game.

Add to this the recent trend within certain members of the scientific community to label our current geological period as the Anthropocene—a period in the earth's history when the human community now controls everything and where Wilderness is no longer a valid construct—and those of us in the Wilderness camp, so to speak, become even smaller. This particular group is unique, as its core philosophy is that we will never reverse the human triumph over nature and that our role today is to become better gardeners of what we have, tending it for human ends and human needs. It's a stewardship role, and to believers in the Anthropocene, Wilderness for Wilderness's sake is naïve and without scientific merit. Stop believing in these antiquated notions, folks; nature is for people.

Just upstream from our campsite is a verdant little spot where we decide to spend the afternoon, reading and nature journaling. Angela has brought a box of watercolors and colored pencils, and given the lack of bright colors in this early spring landscape, we are soon competing over the various hues of green and brown we both need to interpret yellowroot, various levels of branch and log decay, fungi, angelica and unfurling cinnamon ferns. We eventually settle into a sweet accord and spend a couple of hours nestled within this small sanctuary of emergent life. I'm not much of an artist, but I enjoy the meditative aspect of studying something like the frond of a fern, or the colors of angelica, in great detail.

After two days, we have still seen no one. The faint Snowbird Creek Trail will be grown over in a month, and only a few of the hardiest fishermen might make it upstream this far. When Snowbird was declared a Wilderness Study Area by Congress in 1984, it teed the area up for a future Wilderness bill, and the Forest Service basically walked away from it. Dwindling recreation budgets have led many trail systems such as Snowbird's to be abandoned, and without a local volunteer club to maintain them, they are soon overgrown in an area that can receive one hundred inches of rain a year. The area's remoteness is also a factor. Though there is a small trail map available of the area, most people traveling in from urban places to hike would be intimidated by the dead-end roads and beat-up house trailers, street signs in Cherokee syllabary and the mischaracterization of mountain people through Hollywood films like *Deliverance* and the more recent Discovery Channel's *Moonshiners*.

If they had read Peter Jenkins's characterization of the county in his *A Walk Across America*, they might decide it best to never cross the county line. Jenkins entered Graham via the Appalachian Trail, seeking work and companionship as he recorded his National Geographic–sponsored walk for the magazine and his future book. He was quickly characterized as a hippie drug dealer who had come into the county to corrupt the local youth. His harrowing weeklong account of attempting to escape the county while waiting on wired money ended with an implied threat of hanging by the local sheriff. This was over thirty years ago, and though the provincialism and mistrust of outsiders remain, today the most popular restaurant in town is El Pacifico, a Mexican restaurant packed on any given night with locals who reflect anything but xenophobia as they smile and joke with the darker-skinned and English-challenged servers who bring them alcohol-free margaritas and sweet iced tea.

If I were to ask any of them what they thought of more Wilderness for Graham County, I'd likely get a negative response. Many of them would feel that there is an overabundance of federal land here and that the best outcome for their economy would be to sell some of it—or to sell it all. If one of them happened to be one of the few local loggers left here, I'd likely be treated like I was crazy. Then again, I might be told why not, since they don't feel they have enough access to it anyway and never will. At one public Forest Service meeting in Graham County, one of the small sawmill owners in Robbinsville told me that he had to go to other counties to buy timber and pointed out the absurdity to me since 80 percent of Graham County is federally owned. He was a young man whose family had started the business, and when I told him who I worked for, I received no hostility. In fact, he seemed willing to talk and invited me out to his sawmill. At a future meeting, we talked again, and when I told him I thought we could work together, he was very accommodating.

It didn't feel right though. I was an outsider, and it was clear to him and to me that there was an enormous gulf between us in both our historical and current perspectives. I will never know what it is like to have grown up in this remote and provincial place with such deep generational ties to the land, where many of the most elderly still remember the Forest Service buying much of the cutover county in the 1930s and '40s. But people like me aren't going away, and as the local population leaves (Graham County is one of the few western North Carolina counties losing population and has the highest unemployment rate in the state), outsiders will be what replaces them, and they will likely not be as respectful of local culture and traditions as I consider myself to be. In a social ecology study performed not far from here in Macon County where I live, local perspectives were juxtaposed with newcomers, mostly from Florida. One of the most striking examples of conflicting perspectives was that of the newcomers wanting to post their property with No Trespassing and Private Property signs. Locals interviewed couldn't believe that they could no longer walk across a field or hunt the local woods without retribution.

I'd seen these conflicts in my own backyard between my out-of-state neighbors and local bear hunters and had heard numerous complaints by them of the way local people didn't keep their yards cleaned up enough and left junk piled about. I don't want to be perceived this way and want to work with Graham County people to figure out how to protect places like Snowbird and still get timber off the local national forest without destroying its last big wild places. And I want to help keep people out of here who don't respect local traditions like bear hunting, ginseng harvesting, moonshining and freedom to roam the woods as if they were the commons. But it will be a tough road. Most people here believe that a proposed four-lane will bring them economic prosperity, or at least the DOT has convinced them of that, though evidence points to the contrary. If Graham Countians don't like outside attitudes, the last thing they need is a four-lane to cut straight into the heart of their rural landscape, bringing with it low-wage jobs with outside ownership. Not to mention the environmental damage done to this last great dark spot on the map.

Big Snowbird Creek will soon be full of spring rains. We're walking out ahead of them and listening to a Blackburnian warbler as we go. It's thin and high pitched, and I can barely hear it above the wind. Angela can't hear it at all, so maybe I don't really hear it either. Maybe all that matters is the wanting to hear it. I don't know when I'll be back to Big Snowbird again or when I'll have the time again to stop like this for a few days. This barely discernible path will be completely grown over in a few more weeks, and there is a high likelihood that no one will attempt to make this journey down into the Big Snowbird headwaters for the remainder of the spring and summer. I'm glad the coyotes are here, as perhaps they will keep the trails open enough to see where to put my feet the next time I have an opportunity to venture into this largely pathless land. "There, that was a Blackburnian warbler that time," I say, but Angela shakes her head and walks on up the path toward home.

HUNTING FOR CAMELLIAS
AT HORSESHOE BEND

On a small bluff along the Little Tennessee River, just above the point where the river's free-flowing journey from the mountains of North Georgia ends at North Carolina's Fontana Reservoir, is a colony of one of the rarest of Appalachian shrubs, the mountain camellia (*Stewartia ovata*). These plants reside within one of Appalachia's wildest remaining landscapes, with over thirty miles of protected river upstream from them and the storied expanse of the Great Smoky Mountains National Park to their north. To their west and east lies a concentration of national forest land that is unparalleled in its ruggedness and remoteness within the southern Appalachian chain. This is the ancient heartland of the Cherokee people, and not far to the northeast of here, on reservation lands, lies the remainder of their great nation.

I am here today at this remote location with Jack Johnston, an emergency room nurse from Rabun County, Georgia, who is showing me the location of these camellias so we can see them in full bloom. Their existence would remain largely insignificant and unknown were it not for the efforts of Jack, a botanical atavist who tracks their lives meticulously and without interruption. It is an effort that follows on the four-hundred-year history of New World exploration, exploration that involves the documenting of plant and tree species along with their life cycles and propagation.

Jack had written to me earlier in June, inviting me to spend a morning with him looking at a location of mountain camellias that should be in peak bloom. I had heard of the species, but from where I hailed in the northwest

Georgia mountains, I had never seen them or given them a passing thought. I was immediately interested in going with Jack, as I knew that by day's end my knowledge of the species would be enriched greatly. In truth, I was as interested in him and his attraction to this species as anything. He is a rare specimen himself—intense, steady, with layers unknown. How he became such a specimen, I would discover, was the result of the earth he had sprouted from as a boy in Alabama.

During the forty-five-minute drive to our camellia walk, I learn from Jack that he was raised on a subsistence farm in the northeastern corner of Alabama, near the town of Scottsboro. It was not an easy life; poverty was pervasive at the time, and cash was rare. I ask him about his early attraction to plants and nature, and he explains:

> *What made my life different was being the only boy in a family that was geographically isolated living in a cove off the Cumberland Plateau. Traversing the three-hour walk to the top of the plateau, there were no houses near the edge and no children of like age. There was one other farm in the valley floor, and there was a boy who lived there who was my age. He was the son of a sharecropper and did not have much curiosity about anything. We would sometimes walk the fields collecting Indian artifacts that the plows had brought to the surface, but we had little in common.*

The experience was not unlike my own. Though I did not grow up in such a secluded location, it was nonetheless rural, and I, too, had few children nearby who shared my curiosity of the natural world. Except for an occasional hunting excursion with my stepfather or with a boy close to my age who lived at the end of a long gravel road near my home, much of my time in the surrounding forest was spent alone. These solitary days were deeply formative and gave me such a sense of wonder and respect for nature that I have spent most of my adult life working in environmental conservation. This is the reason I am living in the mountains of western North Carolina today and the reason I am friends with Jack.

When I first moved to this rural area, I knew only a handful of people, and though my wife and I were fortunate enough to move into a mountain hollow where the local family accepted us much as their own, my time outdoors was often alone or with my wife. I spent solitary hours hiking in the mountains around us or canoed with my wife on the Little Tennessee River, where we grew closer in our isolation and more creative in our free time. I was anxious to meet others who were also curious about the natural world, and when I told a friend in nearby Rabun County that I was looking for an expert birder to lead a birding event I was planning, he gave me Jack's name without a moment's hesitation.

Jack has no specific formal training in ornithology, botany or ecology, but his undergraduate degree in biology reflects his love of science and his desire to understand the basic building blocks of life. His early years had hardwired him for a life of interest in the natural world. When asked to reflect upon this period, he is quick to reply:

With time alone, I entertained myself by watching birds. I had never seen a bird book to know names but knew the different ones by appearance. The same went for trees. I did learn the names of trees because it was common knowledge for boys to learn which trees were good for lumber and other uses. Observation of detail was how I passed the time. It did not matter what was being observed—a nice tree, a special piece of agate, a bird, snake or other animal. What was important was to observe correctly. In time, it became possible to look at any scene and determine what was different about it. When walking into unfamiliar woods, I would pick out new trees and bushes by looking not at what was ordinary but at what was unusual. These are the skills that made it second nature to begin my observations of the elusive mountain camellius that are found on rare occasions in niche habitats in the mountains. One simply looks for what stands out in an otherwise ordinary landscape.

As we travel on toward this elusive species, the landscape unfolds as anything but ordinary. The river carves its way through a valley floor that is hemmed in by the rugged Nantahala Mountains on one side and the Cowee Mountains on the other. The great American naturalist William Bartram, writing in his *Travels*, described the area in 1775 as "one of the most charming natural mountainous landscapes perhaps anywhere to be seen," as well as one that inspired in him a sublime sense of awe and terror. I had accessed this area in the past by bushwhacking my way in from the other side, for no other reason than to explore what appeared to be a remote spot on the river. With thirty-five miles of the river now protected by the State of North Carolina and the Land Trust for the Little Tennessee, it remains among the most protected rivers of its size in the southern Appalachians.

This is a lonely place, and as a lover of lonely places, I am glad to be here. I sense that Jack is also a fan of such areas and that our common childhood might have something to do with it. I have always felt that I might be closer to the true nature of the world when in lonely places: the emptiness I experience when in such places is liberating. Jack, too, is a fan of the beauty of emptiness. A lifelong student of meditation (given his observations as a child, lifelong is not an overstatement), he currently lives on acreage adjacent to the Center for Spiritual Awareness, where Roy Davis, the last living disciple of Yogananda, resides and instructs people from around the world in meditation techniques. I have also wondered if Jack's meditation practice and disciplined approach to botanical discovery were in part due to the grueling job that he has had for almost two decades in a rural hospital. Years of workdays filled with drug overdoses, automobile accidents, suicide attempts, domestic violence and everything in between have left him with a jaundiced perspective on humanity. Many is the trip where a suicide or drug overdose has been part of the day's ruminations while, far from civilization, we rambled beneath piercing blue sky drinking in shadow-filled winter light. Perhaps the plant world and valleys like the one we will soon be walking into are all that remain of what might be experienced as whole, sacred and worthy of attention.

At the end of the gravel road where we begin our walk, we both comment on the odd assortment of garbage strewn about. Empty beer cartons and bottles, spent rifle and shotgun shells, food wrappers, baby diapers and condom wrappers lay scattered about a grimy and depressing little campsite. Despite the state's efforts to close the place to camping and attendant revelry, the fact that this area lies within one of the most remote corners of Swain County, coupled with inadequate enforcement capacity, ensures that conditions are unlikely to change soon. I describe to Jack how the previous summer, I had stood fishing upriver from the functional swinging bridge we are now crossing while a drunk camper fired a pistol at a sagging and decrepit Bluetick hound baying from the bridge's opposite end.

Here is where the river bends into a perfect horseshoe as it carves its way through rugged mountainous terrain, where geology has given it no other option: Horseshoe Bend—now a geographical place name of a long-abandoned community. Old stone foundations lay scattered about in an overgrown and moss-covered condition, and the area is now completely forested, with large trees growing in its roadbeds and fields. However, on a postcard from the early twentieth century, Horseshoe Bend is largely cleared in pasture, with the spot we are heading to standing out as forested and more rugged.

Given how intolerant of disturbance native, non-cultivar camellias are, the question is how they survived the community that once cleared the land

Horseshoe Bend, Little Tennessee River. *1913 postcard.*

and settled here. Perhaps the camellias lay dormant for many years while the community enjoyed its brief moment here of a hundred or so years. Or perhaps more remarkably, the plants coexisted while the surrounding area was cleared, cut and quarried. Regardless, their sensitive existence in this location has continued for at least sixty or seventy years, as is determined by their size and slow-growing nature. Jack explains that the mountain camellia is limited to specific habitat niches, which he does his best to describe to me. The plant is usually (but not always) found near water and in acidic soil. Good drainage is required, and the mountain camellia is always found on slopes, usually rugged and rock-strewn. He has observed that in certain forest types, the mountain camellia is never found, regardless of the growing conditions, adding further to the mysterious nature of the species.

The recognition of the species at all must be credited to William Bartram. Traveling westward in 1775 from Charleston up colonial trading paths to the mountains of western North Carolina, Bartram was our earliest chronicler of both cultural and natural history in this part of Appalachia. Upon his entry into the mountains, Bartram, an astute observer and illustrator of plant and animal life, filled his notebooks with descriptions of species new to Europeans. One of these species was *Stewartia ovata*, or mountain camellia, which he first encountered approximately seventy miles from here, in the

Jack Johnston with mountain camellia flower, Overflow Creek. *Photo by Brent Martin.*

mountains of modern-day Oconee County, South Carolina. Being familiar with our only other native camellia, the extremely rare coastal variety *Stewartia malacodendron*, or silky camellia, Bartram immediately recognized the mountain camellia as a new species. The rarity of the mountain camellia at the time is uncertain, but today, the species is found only in a handful of locations, primarily in western North Carolina and the mountainous portions of adjacent states. The State of North Carolina considers the plant's official status as "imperiled."

Both *Stewartia* are closely related to *Franklinia alatamaha* (Franklin tree, now extinct in the wild), and all are members of the family Theaceae. *Franklinia* exists today only as a result of Bartram's discovery of it in 1763 along the Altamaha River in southeast Georgia. It had not been found again in the wild since May 1803, when botanist John Lyon found several of the plants growing at or near Bartram's original location for the species: Fort Barrington in Georgia. Bartram's fascination with the species, his collection of its seed and subsequent propagation is the only reason we have any knowledge of it at all. Given its rarity in the eighteenth century, its demise most likely occurred following the clearing of its habitat for cotton farming and the inadvertent and attendant introduction of the waterborne disease phytophthora.

I ask Jack about the mountain camellia's rarity and its relationship to *Franklinia* and possible ice age impacts to the distribution of both species. As Jack describes the possibilities, there are some who think that *Franklinia* was never found widely and that it had been pushed into the coastal plain during the last ice age, when it grew non-contiguously until its demise. According to this theory, *Franklinia* would have perhaps been an Appalachian species prior to the ice age, migrating to warmer climates as the mountains grew colder. Part of the reasoning behind this theory is that *Franklinia* seems to do so well in mountain landscaping today. Specimens growing on my small mountain farm exceed twelve feet in height.

Perhaps the mountain camellia was also severely impacted by the ice age and remained in a severely restricted range as a result. Or, as Jack suggests,

Franklinia alatamaha, by William Bartram. *Courtesy of the Natural History Museum, London.*

maybe it is simply at the end of its evolutionary lifespan. Regardless of the explanation, it is interesting that all three North American members of the Theaceae family are rare and restricted in their range. Given Jack's personal physical restriction of range in his early years, I am also interested in what attracted him to this plant in the first place, particularly since it did not grow in his childhood forest. Jack explains that he first saw *Stewartia malacodendron* on the cover of a coffee table book in Alabama, where this particular species is found in a handful of locations on the coastal plain. A friend of Jack's who had spent his childhood roaming the creek banks where it is found knew of the plants from his grandfather, and he arranged to walk with Jack to view the blooms one May afternoon. "I was impressed that something so beautiful was to be found in remote woods far from human activity," Jack tells me as we cross the river and reach the shore. "Later, I came to realize that habitat undisturbed by the heavy hand of man is the preferred site for these plants."

As we proceed to their location, Jack explains how the species reproduces slowly and yet produces an abundance of seed. Much like Bartram's efforts with propagating *Franklinia*, Jack's own efforts at propagating its cousin, the mountain camellia, are legendary. No one has experimented more than Jack with growing this plant from seeds and cuttings—which is indeed part of the reason why we are here. When the shrub is blooming is the time to take cuttings and attempt to root them in containers. Jack has had consistent success with this technique, as have I, after his patient instruction and assistance.

When we arrive, the camellias are loaded with blooms, and Jack is ecstatic. It is a spectacular sight, and I am grateful to be present with this rare individual as he experiences a rapturous moment among these unfolding white beauties. Camellias have a relatively short blooming period, and within two weeks, the blossoms will fade and drop to the forest floor. During this time, Jack will visit as many locations as possible, evaluating and comparing the blooms with last year's and deciding where he will return in the fall to collect seeds. We spend a good hour there as Jack chooses the perfect cuttings from this year's most vigorous new growth, placing them gently in moist Ziploc bags until they can be taken home to be dipped in the rooting hormone and placed immediately in soil.

From here, we take a brief hike around the rugged bluff above, looking hard for additional specimens—with no success. He has found them only on this side of the river and only in a couple of additional locations upriver from here. As we scramble down the steep hillside, I am suddenly reminded of the work of Michael Pollan, who, in his *Botany of Desire* (Random House,

Mountain camellia at the author's home. *Photo by Angela Faye Martin.*

2001), argues that through their own need for survival, plants have actually domesticated us, rather than the reverse. Has the beauty of this rare mountain species worked its charms in such a way that it has found in Jack a guaranteed propagator for its survival?

As we follow the gravel road back out, I drive slowly, occasionally stopping while Jack peers through binoculars as deeply as he can into the slopes and ravines that drain into Sawmill Creek. We have not traveled far when Jack spots a snowy white patch not far off the road. It is a new location, and as we excitedly exit the car, Jack remarks that there could be more locations up these little side drainages—an invitation to future explorations. Interestingly, the stamens of the specimens on this side of the river are purple, in stark contrast to the white stamens on the opposite side of the river. There is no apparent reason for this except that the forest is slightly different here, with its Frasier magnolia, white oak and two or more species of pine.

After a half hour or so of observation and the careful selection of cuttings, we leave and agree to come back in the fall to collect seeds. This is an annual and important affair for Jack. His fall pilgrimage involves a wide circumnavigation of North Georgia, Alabama and western North Carolina, where he collects thousands of seeds, which are carefully organized by location, stamen color and any other notable characteristics. He then stratifies the seeds for later propagation or mails them to a West Coast nursery that is working with him on wholesale propagation.

Jack explains his approach to the tedious problem of raising both species of camellia:

> *I think that if we assume that all knowledge is always present and that at times something can become known that was not previously known, we can receive answers. For example, a question posed to the universal mind, if presented in stillness, can often be answered. I have seen this situation many, many times in basic science research. If the right person poses the correct question in a manner that allows an answer, then an answer comes. It may be slow, but it does seem to work. When you look at Sri Yukteswar, an early twentieth-century yogi, he alluded to an understanding of electromagnetism that was unknown to science in his day. He stated that this would become common knowledge sometime in the future, and that would be the time for it to unfold.*

Mental sketches such as this are what I have come to expect from Jack when discussing our abilities to understand the natural world. His is a forest manner that utilizes silent and meditative contemplation. He further describes his own unfolding:

> *When it comes to growing* Stewartia, *I think that some things can be learned. You and I have both learned a lot. More remains. Isn't it interesting that we have a chance to work on this? What has happened with me in regards to inquiring about* Stewartia *is that I have first looked at what occurs in the wild. Slope and aspect and the fact that the seeds sprout where a steep slope meets a flatter slope seem critical, as the leaves provide a better mulch and moisture layer. Then one looks at shade to realize that canopy gaps are the very best locations for this plant and that little ones with too much shade never prosper until the right light occurs. As one learns more, the knowledge comes in interesting ways. I look forward to continuing my learning about something as long as I can.*

Given that he has spent twenty years acquiring knowledge of the species, this is not a statement to take lightly. Also interesting is that this slow and scientific method of propagation has resulted in additional observations by Jack about those individuals who pursue the arcana of plant collecting. Most serious Appalachian plant propagators know of Jack's success with the species and seek him out for landscaping specimens, seed and information. His illustrative and rather jaundiced view of this aspect of his work is revealing:

> *No one seemed interested in my work with the species until success was evident. Then there was a mad rush to get plants. My perception was that people thought they could order plants like they would order fast food at a drive-through window. Because they had a request, the expectation was that it be met. They had no interest at all in the years required to produce plants ten inches tall, of the tick bites, briar scratches, sore muscles, wet feet and occasional dehydration that resulted from long ventures into the habitat of the species. They wanted a plant that was going to perform in their landscape as they expected it to perform. There was little consideration for the requirements of the species. One attitude was that it was expected to have a regular, beautiful form that grew rapidly and produced a multitude of flowers each spring season. This was supposed to occur with no particular effort on the part of the grower.*

Jack characterizes two groups of people who have acquired plants from him: those who listened to his approach on growing the plant and those who did not. Successful ones sited their plants with afternoon shade, mulched around the roots to keep them cooler and patiently allowed the plants to grow slowly. Unsuccessful ones heeded little of his advice, and when a request was made for a replacement, he would suggest that the person making the request instead go through the steps that he had used to get another plant. As he tells it, "this caused an immediate lack of interest and settled the matter."

With regard to his botanical "atavism," we have had many such seekers in the southern Appalachians—those who arrived here nomadically thousands of years ago and created worlds of sanctity out of the plants and animals they observed and those who arrived in the post-Columbian New World and marveled at the unknown, staggering richness and diversity. For any denizen of Appalachia, the plant world is an expression of color and dream; in winter it is a deep sleeper, one that wakes to bring forth a spectrum of vivid luminosity that a seeker of such richness may walk and revel in. Perhaps at one time we all lived within this luminosity.

Though this long tradition appears to be a dying one, and though our wild world seems to fade a little more each day, we are fortunate that seekers of such rarities persevere. And bearing witness to these seekers is an opportunity to learn how such searches become a means to personal fulfillment. My experience is that seekers such as Jack become a type of container—a vessel that preserves and expresses the essence of the wild and rare thing. And for many who know them, their perspectives become a blessing—a thing to be marveled at alongside the rare and observed.

On one of our winter trips to Horseshoe Bend the following year, Jack and I decide to go far upriver on the opposite side from the original location. Looking at a USGS topographical map, there appear to be some interesting bluffs and small drainages there that are great candidates for new camellia locations. It is a very cold afternoon, well below freezing, brilliant blue, and as we walk, Jack closely scouts the forest. As we skirt a small bend in the river, we see a large whitetail doe entering the river below us. She is alone, does not see us above her on this high bluff, and for a good half hour we follow along quietly and watch her as she swims upstream, stopping at every rocky shoal to shake and look about.

It is such a bitter cold day that we can find no explanation as to why she would go for such a long and painful swim. We stand there in the cold for a long time watching her until she at last exits the river and stands basking in the sunshine on the opposite bank. Why would this deer go for such a swim in this cold dark river, we ask, as we shiver and shuffle about? Why would any deer go on such a seemingly meaningless swim in this cold and lonely river? The doe glances about, eases into a thick band of rhododendron and fetterbush and then disappears.

THE DIVIDING SPRING

There is another world under this, and it is like ours in everything—animals, plants, and people—save that the seasons are different. The streams that come down from the mountains are the trails by which we reach this underworld, and the springs at their heads are the doorways by which we enter it, but to do this one must fast and go to water and have one of the underground people for a guide. We know that the seasons in the underworld are different from ours because the water in the springs is always warmer in the winter and cooler in summer than the outside air.
—*from James Mooney's* History, Myths, and Sacred Formulas
of the Cherokees, *1891*

Within the heart of the southern Appalachian Mountains, where the Cowee, Nantahala and Blue Ridge Mountains converge, lies a rich tapestry of human and natural history woven over the millennia from myriad interactions between the plant, animal and inanimate worlds. It is the homeland of the Cherokee people, whose cosmology is a layered interpretation of the complexity of season and geography, the explosion of spring from the gray and stark shadowy world of winter and the incalculable number of birth and death experiences within one of the oldest mountain ranges on earth. And it is a land of water—water that is present throughout the landscape in powerful and profound display. Mysterious springs bubble forth in small and hidden grottos; waterfalls cascade down narrow and impassable gorges; rivers carve their way through wide and alluvial valleys. As it has shaped this land, so has it shaped the consciousness of its inhabitants.

The journey leading me to these ancient mountains begins with the springs that emerged from the hollows surrounding my boyhood home in the once-wild forests of Cobb County, Georgia. One spring that I have a particularly strong memory of was located near an abandoned old farmstead where I squirrel hunted and would stop for cool drinks after long autumn and winter sojourns. It was marked by a large spring box, made of roughly worked square stones fitted perfectly into the hillside, its setting completed with a large beech tree full of pocketknife doodles and arborglyphic strangeness. A quartz arrowhead once emerged from the loose soil near its edge, my first such find, which has motivated me to this day to pay attention to the soil beneath my feet. The spring is now gone, submerged beneath a terminal landscape of oversized suburban homes and decaying strip malls, along with every vestige of that once-rich cultural landscape. I will never know its history nor whether the Cherokees who once inhabited that sacred place revered it or knew it by name.

However, I am hopeful that this is not the story of the spring that I and three equally interested friends are searching for today. Located near the tiny town of Mountain City in the extreme northeastern corner of Georgia, the spring is said to flow from a point below the spine of the Eastern Continental Divide, where the Blue Ridge Mountains drop to a low point of 2,044 feet. This wide and low-lying gap is so indistinguishable that were it not for a sign on State Highway 441 signifying its crossing, most travelers would never give it a passing thought. In an 1892 report from the chief of engineers to the U.S. Army, which was then considering a canal through the gap, it is described as "one of the most remarkable depressions in the Blue Ridge…and to the traveler passing along this road, it has the appearance of a narrow valley separating two parallel ridges, rather than a gap in a great dividing ridge."

Eighteenth-century explorers mapped and described the gap as a marshy savannah, but today it is a tomato field of several acres that spreads behind a short row of storefronts where bronzed Hispanic workers bend to the task of harvesting under a dazzling autumn sky. On this particular October day, the town is silent but for the endless and steady drone of automobiles and tractor trailers, which occupy this ancient major north–south pathway both night and day.

The significance of this spring is derived from the fact that for many thousands of years its waters flowed down into this wide and shallow area where it mingled with waters of other springs, leaving on its journey in opposite directions into two major river basins. Water flowing south from this point winds its way for several miles to the southeast to join the Chattooga River—the rugged mountain setting of James Dickey's controversial novel and film *Deliverance*—where it flows on to the Savannah River and the Atlantic Ocean. Water flowing north forms the Little Tennessee River, which makes its way into the Tennessee River and the Gulf of Mexico.

This is a rare and interesting geographical and geological phenomenon, but the cultural overlay is equally intriguing. To the colonial traders who settled among the Cherokees in the area, the spring was enchanted. This belief was first chronicled by the noted Indian trader James Adair, who passed through the area in 1775 and wrote a vivid description of the spring's mythical powers in his classical work *History of the American Indians*. By Adair's account, one drink from its waters and the recipient would lose his or her ability to leave and would spend the next seven years living within the wilds of the ancient Blue Ridge Mountains. This belief was also documented by ethnographer James Mooney, who described the spring in his *Sacred Myths and Formulas of the Cherokee Indians* in 1891.

However, the name that was bestowed upon it after its first documented European encounter was Herbert's Spring, named after Commissioner of Indian Affairs John Herbert, who traveled through the valley in late 1727 and early 1728 and later mapped the Carolinas in 1744. Though Herbert's journal from the period makes no mention of the spring, Herbert spent several months in the area, meeting with Cherokee headmen and attempting to rouse them against the Lower Creeks, who had committed several attacks on colonials near the Altamaha River in southern Georgia. One can only speculate that Herbert must have described the area's geographical features somewhere in some detail, with this significant gap and spring registering with particular vividness in his consciousness. Herbert's Savannah, however, does not show up formally on a map until 1764, when British army officer and historian Thomas Mante mapped the area in great detail.

Mante's map shows Herbert's Savannah and spring prominently on the map. It is drawn in as a large savannah, signifying the low-lying marsh that existed there before the era of draining, channelizing and filling. America's great naturalist William Bartram also passed through the gap in 1775, and though he does not mention Herbert's Spring or the savannah, he describes in some of the most rapturous language of the time the location's lush meadows, waterfalls and streams.

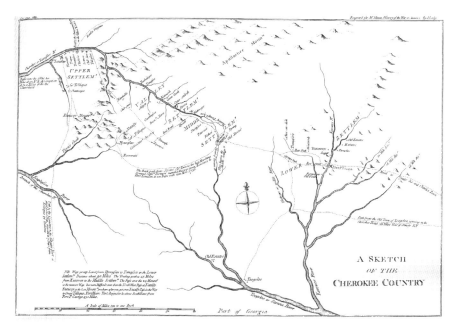

Cherokee Country, 1764, by British cartographer Thomas Mante. Herbert's Savannah is clearly demarcated near the center of the map. *Courtesy of Pennsylvania State University, Special Collections Library.*

Well over two hundred years later, there are four of us who are passing through this gap in search of the remains of its rich history. Dr. Tom Hatley is the recent past chair of Cherokee Studies at Western Carolina University and author of *Dividing Paths*, a seminal work on Cherokee people and their interactions with colonial South Carolina settlers. Tom has corresponded with me for some time now about the significance and possible location of the spring. He tells us that there is only one other such spring in the eastern United States and that its significance was so profound that the two tribes that were connected to it culturally had refused to include it in land session treaties in the early nineteenth century.

Carrie McLachlan teaches Native American history at Western Carolina University and is in the final stages of a dissertation on Cherokee Indian religion. She is meticulous in her search for the spring's location, and she and Lamar Marshall pore over the maps like bloodhounds, searching for every geographical and topographical nuance, determined to place us in the proper location. Lamar works as cultural heritage director for the nonprofit organization Wild South, where he works to identify and protect cultural heritage sites.

We have determined that a prominent spring on the USGS map for the area is our most likely candidate. The spring is noted as Darling Spring, and it sits astride the divide in a well-defined nook that should not be hard to locate, especially since Darling Spring Road is one of the few roads that make up the town's small intersection. We drive the road out slowly until we determine that we are in the curve of the road where the spring should be located. An older home sits directly across the road from where we believe the spring to be, tucked away and invaded by an overgrown thicket of nonnative privet and multiflora rose.

Just to the west of the spring, a modern new home sits in a manicured and well-hidden setting. The gravel road that parallels the drainage the spring bubbles forth from is a string of broken-down single-wide trailers and dilapidated automobiles. Uncertain as to whether we are in the right place, we push our way through the thicket to where we believe the spring to be. It is only a few yards through before we see a small PVC pipe emerging from beneath the soil, where water flows steadily in this record-setting debilitating drought. Despite our excitement, it is a depressing little sight with all of the exotic vegetation and the worn-out and eroding hillside above us.

We decide it best to inform the locals as to what we are up to, so I advance to the older home in hopes of meeting the occupants. The woman who greets me warily becomes more curious once I spew out our strange inquiry and explains that her husband is busy but will be out soon to talk with us. I decide to approach the owner of the much larger new home while we wait on Mr. Dotson. The owner is immediately interested in our excursion and explains in an accent that is not of this place that the spring is on his property and that we are welcome to explore, and would we like something cold to drink on this warm October day?

We climb back into the privet thicket and quickly find above the spring pipe a brick-tiled floor that is covered with a carpet of Vinca and English ivy. It clearly was a significant location in more modern times, and the path to such disrepair and insignificance is a mystery. At about this point, we see Mr. Dotson emerge from his home and amble toward us, squinting in the bright sunlight. He is maybe seventy years old, maybe a little older, and tells us he has lived here all his life. We explain our search for the spring, and he seems mildly impressed that anyone would care. He explains that the spring was once a gathering place where people would come to get water and that a pavilion once protected it, of which we have clearly found the floor today. According to Mr. Dotson, it has always been called Darling Spring, but when

I ask him if he has ever heard it referred to as Herbert's Spring, he shifts and cocks his head and says, "Yeah, I have," in a way that has a slight amount of uncertainty in it.

However, as we study the maps closer, along with Adair's description of its location, we become increasingly certain that Darling Spring, despite its significance, is not Herbert's Spring. Adair's original description reads:

> From the head of the southern branch of Savannah river it does not exceed half a mile to a head spring of the Mississippi water that runs through the middle and upper parts of the Cherokee nation about a northwest course, and, joining other rivers, they empty themselves into the great Mississippi. The above fountain is called "Herbert's spring," so named from an early commissioner of Indian affairs, and it was natural for strangers to drink thereof, to quench thirst, gratify their curiosity, and have it to say they had drank of the French waters.

Since we have determined that Darling Spring is clearly a head branch of the Savannah, Herbert's Spring and the once French waters of the Mississippi must lie somewhere within a half mile to the north.

On our second trip to the area, we return to examine the large area where the savannah would have been had it not been ditched, drained and filled. It is a spectacular autumn day, and we decide to stop and ask the workers who are finishing up the tomato harvest if we might walk around the large field for a bit. I determine with my broken Spanish that the jefe of this group leases the field and has no problem with us walking about. The low-lying area is ringed with watery ditches and one bold small stream that bisects the area. Hatley examines a bit of clay that he describes as common to hydric soils, which signifies historical water coverage. River cane, once abundant and culturally significant to the Cherokees, is attempting to creep back in, though it will have a difficult time with the constant clearing and alteration of water flow.

Back in the car, we follow the divide's undulating contours around to where we find a large stream on our topographical map called Black's Creek that flows out of a deep hollow and clearly is a headwater stream of the Little Tennessee River. We stop to look at a small pond that is full in this record drought and a small stream that feeds it. It is next to a rambling old mountain home, which was most likely located here for the constant flow of clean water. We also visit another farm that happens to have a small sign out front that reads "Tennvannah Farm." A small but bold stream parallels the driveway, and since the home sits next to the old trade path that is now State Highway 441, it is a good candidate. We drive up the gravel road slowly, and when we reach the farmhouse at its end, we find its occupants are not home and decide it best to leave instead of taking the liberty to walk around.

Traveling slowly back for one last look at the Darling Spring and the drive beyond it, we search the slopes for what might be another spring. It is record drought, but surely such a significant spring would have some water or moisture to mark its origin. If the Darling Spring were the head of the southern branch of the Savannah River, then Herbert's Spring must lie somewhere within the drive we have just made out to Black's Creek and the Tennvannah Farm.

On the drive back to Darling Spring, we drive slowly and look closely at the pastureland just to the north. About a half mile north of the spring, we all remark upon a small pond of about twenty feet in length that lies perched on a hillside with no apparent water source. A coppice of scruffy trees obscures our view, and since we cannot see it closely, we are uncertain as to whether this is a spring. It is getting late in the day, so we must return for a third visit.

When I return home, I e-mail Carrie to ask her about her interest in the spring. She tells me that her interest lies in what she is working on with her dissertation and sends the following excerpt from what she has written, which includes a quotation from noted nineteenth-century librarian and historian Charles Lanman's *Letters from the Alleghany Mountains* (1854):

> *Long ago, a Cherokee Headman, Kostoyeak, Sharp Shooter, fell in love with a Yamasee maiden. But because of her great beauty and family connections she was desired by many suitors of various tribes. Her father, a Yamasee chief, devised a contest to try the suitors. The man who succeeded in finding the common source of the two great river systems that flowed in opposite directions from the continental divide, the Savannah River and the Tennessee River, would marry this Yamasee maiden. According to Lanman's account, Kostoyeak succeeded in finding the source at "a gorge—now called the gap of the Blue Ridge as well as Rabun Gap—where the two great rivers 'shake hands and commence their several journeys.'"*

Such accounts as Lanman's, as well as Adair's and Mooney's, seized the imagination of nineteenth-century American fiction writer Mary Noailles Murfree (1850–1922), who wrote under the pseudonym Charles Egbert

Craddock. In the March 1900 issue of *Harper's*, Murfree published "A Victor at Chungke," a fictional account of the Cherokee ball game Chungke and attendant colonial traders during the difficult Cherokee years following the French and Indian War. In describing one such trader and his life among the Cherokees, Murfree writes:

> *He was possessed by that extraordinary renunciation of civilization which now and again was manifested by white men thrown among the Cherokee tribe....Whether the wild sylvan life had some peculiarly irresistible attraction; whether the world beyond held for them responsibilities and laborious vocations and irksome ties which they would fain evade; whether they fell under the bewitchment of "Herbert's Spring," after drinking whereof one could not quit the region of the Great Smoky Mountains, but remained in that enchanted country for seven years, fascinated, lapsed in perfect content—it is impossible to say. There is a tradition that when the attraction of the world would begin to reassert its subtle reminiscent forces, these renegades of civilization were wont to repair anew to this fountain to quaff again of the ancient delirium and to revive its potent spell.*

Murfree borrowed heavily from Adair's account from over seventy-five years earlier. Adair's original description of Herbert's Spring, which might have had its own fictional qualities, reads:

> *Some of our people, who went only with the view of staying a short time, but by some allurement or other exceeded the time appointed, at their return reported, either through merriment or superstition, that the spring had such a natural bewitching quality that whosoever drank of it could not possibly quit the nation during the tedious space of seven years. All the debauchees readily fell in with this superstitious notion as an excuse for their bad method of living, when they had no proper call to stay in that country; and in process of time it became as received a truth as any ever believed to have been spoken by the Delphic oracle.*

On the third trip back to the area, only Lamar and I are there from the original crew, but we have picked up another interested party, Honor Woodard, a local painter and photographer who draws inspiration in her work from the cultural and natural history of the area. It is a dreary and soggy day when we gather at the Mountain City post office. A thick cloud bank hangs over the Blue Ridge, and the recently plowed savannah is a wash of mud. We drive up the road to the farm where we think Herbert's Spring might gurgle forth into the small pond that we had noticed on the previous trip. The house that sits at its edge is fairly modern, and though we are doubtful that they are the owners of the spring, it is a place to start.

I am elected spokesperson for the group and so walk to their door alone, a stranger with a strange tale. The woman who greets me is friendly and curious and talks rapidly as I sit before her long bookshelf and collection of old blue Ball Mason jars. Her silent husband appears to be in poor health, and he stares steadily ahead as we talk, sipping from a small carton of low-fat milk while we prattle away about the spring. She seems interested in the history and tells me that the family who owns it is most likely at work. They are the Hooper family, and though she thinks they would have no problem with us walking around, it is after all a farm, and there are dogs and farm animals to consider.

She is so intrigued by the story that she thinks it best to call them at work immediately and see if it is possible for us to take a look around. After a few minutes of chatting, she hands the phone over to me. No, Mrs. Hooper knows nothing about Herbert's Spring but will be happy to have her husband give us a call if we would like to have a look around. We leave, and I agree to return with the story when it is complete. Since we have no permission to look around, we drive back out to the road and park, standing in the rain and peering about for a better view of the dip in the pasture where a small grove of trees sits above the pond where the spring might indeed exist.

After a few minutes, Lamar declares that he thinks the spring is on the other side of the savannah, at Tennvannah Farm, which we have considered before but could not look around due to its owners being absent. He has researched all of the historical maps, and the old trading path through the gap clearly was on the west side of the savannah. It would make sense that travelers passing through would stop to get water and rest at a spring that was close to their path. We drive the road up to the old farmhouse at the top of a knoll and find that it appears to be empty. An old log smokehouse sits on the hill behind it, and a corncrib of similar appearance sits just beyond it. A crew of motley-looking dogs gather about me and sniff.

As I am approaching the door to knock, a small car pulls into the driveway behind me, and a woman of about sixty opens the door to greet me. She is friendly and trusting and invites me in. I am explaining to her why we are there while also thinking that I am entering one of the oldest mountain homes I have ever been in. Sitting at a desk within is Ray Connor, who speaks

Above and opposite: The Dividing Spring. *Photos by Brent Martin.*

with a rugged mountain accent and a friendly grin. He tells me quickly he is a pastor at a Church of God in nearby Hiawassee and that he is only the caretaker, not the owner. He has been there for eleven years though and has studied the place over pretty well. He points to a hill behind the house where the Scruggs family who built the home lies in eternal rest.

The Scruggses built this place in 1825, he says. Cherokee land, I think, only fifty years after Adair and Bartram passed through. Only seventy-five after Herbert himself passed the winter here and claimed it for his name. I tell him about our search for the spring, and he instantly begins telling me of the spring on the property that was renowned for its quality and appearance. It was such a good flow that they made a log flume from it down to the railroad tracks to fill up the trains, he says, as we exit the house to retrieve Lamar and Honor.

The spring is there below the house, in a small amphitheater of stacked stone, gurgling forth on this wet December day much as Herbert himself must have seen it. All of our instinct and research tells us that this is the place. From where the spring leaves the dark earth from beneath large stones, a small circular pool has been carved from rock to serve as a basin. It is perhaps two and a half feet across and six inches deep. Its water is warmer than the outside air, and perhaps there is an underworld beyond

its entrance that we will never know. We kneel to drink from the spring, one at a time. The rain is steady, and the hemlocks and rhododendron sag with days of saturation. We take photos and plan with Mr. Connor for our return for more.

On our way out, we stop to look at an ancient and enormous beech tree just a few yards from the spring, covered in undecipherable scribblings. Lamar thinks it is at least three hundred years old and that with powdered chalk we might interpret some of the carvings grown wide with age. What would we know but could we understand? Did a boy stand here once who pulled artifacts from the soil? Were Herbert's initials somewhere buried in that tree's old gray cambium layer, grown thick with growth and the widening gulf of time?

Two more stops before we drive back home—one to locate a possible Native American ceremonial mound that Mr. Connor has told us of not far down the river, another to partake in the local fare at Country Vittles. We drive to the river and walk downstream through a recently plowed field where old potatoes lie rotting in the mud. Agriculture, houses and roads have taken their toll on the river in this low gradient section, and the steep and collapsing banks are far from their original condition. The rain is growing heavier, but we see what we think is the mound and stare across the river at it and wonder. There are large trees growing from its summit and stones scattered about. Despite our shared knowledge of the mounds within the

Little Tennessee River Valley, we have heard nothing of this mound until today, and we are mystified.

What we know is that this dark and silt-laden river has traveled between these long-worked fields for many, many years and that many have come before us and drank deeply from its source a few miles up the road. There are plans to widen this section of state highway, as they have to the south of here, where Atlanta's sprawling metropolis has pushed growth out deep into these old and majestic mountains. Real concerns abound about Atlanta's need for water and the possibility of interbasin transfers out of the Little Tennessee River. Vacation homes ring the ridgetops, and tourists come from all directions to enjoy the area's national forests and whitewater paddling.

Walking back to the car, I reflect upon my years of living in this magnificent valley and of the layered and rich history that I walk upon and inherit. It feels like home, and like one worth working to protect. Now I have drank from the sacred spring and am perhaps confined to these mountains against my will, but should such hopes begin to fade, I will repair anew to this fountain to quaff again of the ancient delirium and to revive its potent spell.

WHEN THE HEART CAN NO LONGER
SAY HOME

The day will arrive when those afflicted people will not only have full satisfaction for their oppressions, but dreadful irrevocable wrath, when they will be masters and either enslave or exterminate them, their masters and oppressors, unless ye speedily take measures to do them justice by giving them liberty, freedom, thus natural and political right equal to our own maxims and solemn acts and promises in the face of heaven.
—*William Bartram, "Antislavery Treatise," published in* Catalogue of American Trees *(Philadelphia, 1783)*

The confident, digitized woman in the smart phone tells us to exit, so we follow her commands and leave Interstate 81 to run the gauntlet of southwest Philadelphia toward Bartram's Garden, through one of the highest unemployment and crime-ridden areas of the city, past the boarded-up and burned-out row houses, past the wandering homeless and drug-addled adults and onto Lexington Road. Turning right at the public housing project called Bartram Village, we follow the signs down to the entrance for one of the oldest and most significant gardens in America. I'm questioning the artificial woman inside the smart phone for selecting this route, but I'm glad she did. I needed to see the garden from this perspective, this oasis of sweetness lying within a post-industrial wasteland, beckoning.

In 1728, when farmer and botanist John Bartram purchased the original 102 acres that became his masterpiece, the area was pastoral but bustling. The nearby Gray's Ferry carried most of the western and southern traffic across the Schuylkill River into Philadelphia. It would take 150 years before the Industrial Revolution transformed the area into a manufacturing zone and then another hundred until the current era of abandonment and neglect began. Ironically, but not surprisingly, the majority population here is African American. The Bartrams were Quakers, though John Bartram was not opposed to slavery, even attempting to make a planter out of his abolitionist son William, a failed and disastrous endeavor. The Bartrams' early history included John's father being killed by Indians in North Carolina. He never held the sympathetic and unpopular views of his egalitarian son toward America's native peoples because of this. William Bartram's famous 1791 publication *Travels* remains one of the most important cultural documents in existence for its attention to southeastern Indians' customs and traditions.

From where we park, the hazy skyline of Philadelphia is to our east, and from the rise where we begin our walk, we can see the river below us. It's a hot and humid late June day, and my wife is concerned about exertion because before we left our home in western North Carolina my heart became irregular in the middle of the night. Similar episodes over the years have always been brief, and I have never been diagnosed with any heart damage or irregularity. I ameliorate her by promising I will go to the doctor upon our return home, and to the emergency room if it really scares me. But today I'm at Bartram's Garden, a bucket list of American landmarks I have been determined to travel to before I die, oblivious that I am closer to death than I realize.

Uncertain, we proceed toward the cluster of stone buildings that form the centerpiece of the estate. We find the entranceway and follow it to a courtyard where we emerge among potted plants and where two young African American men are working in some horticultural endeavor. We wander a few minutes admiring the plants, some of which are *Franklinia alatamaha*, one of the world's rarest shrubs, long gone from the wild and existing today only due to William Bartram's collection of its seeds from a population he and his father discovered in Georgia's Altamaha River basin in 1765. The young men see us milling about the *Franklinia* and ask if we know about its significance. I explain that we have been growing these for years at our small mountain farm in western North Carolina. This is not something they hear often, I can tell, and they look at me incredulously, cracking wise with humorous doubt. After a few minutes of attempting to convince them, they genially point us toward the gift shop and entrance, and we carry on, paying our entrance fee and purchasing a membership.

The author at Bartram's Garden with what is believed to be the oldest living gingko in North America. It was one of three shipped to the United States from London as a gift from plant collector William Hamilton. The other two, planted nearby in Philadelphia, are no longer alive. *Photo by Angela Faye Martin.*

The week before our departure, nine members of the Emanuel African Methodist Episcopal Church in Charleston, South Carolina, were killed by a gunman during prayer service. The suspect, identified as twenty-one-year-old Dylann Roof, confessed to committing the shooting in hopes of igniting a race war. This horror is swirling within me as I think about the garden here and the long-dead man who led me to it—the lonely abolitionist, pacifist, cultural connoisseur of America's native peoples—William Bartram, personal hero of my homeplace geography and author of a soundly dashed dream of a just society. After committing this heinous act, Roof proceeded toward the mountains of western North Carolina, to what he likely considered a safe haven. And when the Confederate flags began coming down from the South's courthouses following his capture, they began coming up in my bucolic mountain valley. This fact sickens me.

When William Bartram entered my home landscape of Cowee in May 1775, he encountered the remains of the Cherokee culture. Cowee had been devastated by a previous campaign of the French and Indian War

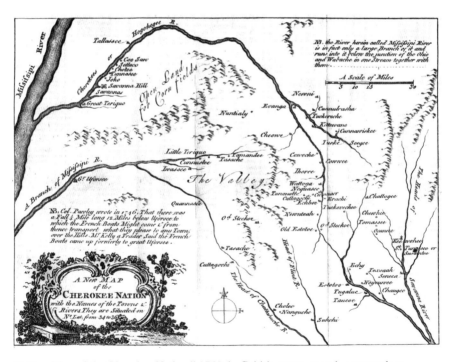

"A New Map of the Cherokee Nation," 1760, by British engraver and cartographer Thomas Kitchin. Engraved for *London Magazine*. *Courtesy of Digital Commonwealth: Massachusetts Collections Online.*

over a decade earlier and had yet to fully recover. Arriving on the eve of the American Revolution, only a little over a year later, Griffith Rutherford would march his troops into Cowee and brutally destroy the town, ensuring against a potential Cherokee alliance with the British. It would be the end of this vibrant political and economic capital of the Middle Town Cherokees. Bartram's account of his visit here is the only intimate portrayal of the Little Tennessee Valley at this time—plant species yet to be described by science, careful observations of Cherokee customs and rapturous descriptions of a landscape profoundly changed in the two-hundred-plus years hence.

We exit the gift shop, maps in hand, to find a small group of young adults gathered about a man who is obviously an employee and a guide. We are determined to horn in on their walkabout. He eventually welcomes us, and we introduce ourselves following his introduction of all those present. They are instructors for the Mighty Writers, an inner-city summer program for kids planning to meet here for daily instruction and connection to nature. I learn later that the mission of Mighty Writers is to combat a 40 percent inner-city high school dropout rate and teach Philadelphia kids "to think and write with clarity so they can achieve success at school, work, and in life."

The author with Bartram's Garden curator Joel Fry. *Photo by Angela Faye Martin.*

Together, we wander on into the remains of William Bartram's vision, into its capacity to heal and transform us. At the point in the tour where we stop to look at the site where the old Eastwick mansion stood, we can see down the hill below us onto rows of vegetables that form the community garden for the surrounding neighborhood. The guide tells us that the garden was created to provide affordable organic food for people who have no access to it otherwise. A garden within a garden, a dream within a dream. The executive director of Bartram's Garden, Maitreyi Roy, refers to the garden as "the outdoor living room of southwest Philadelphia." Yoga and art classes, writing, gardening, nature study and access to the outdoors—all with a focus on serving an underserved community and improving its residents' quality of life. If William Bartram is somewhere out there in the afterlife looking down, I can imagine he is pleased.

During my continuance here, about half an hour, I experienced the most perfect and agreeable hospitality conferred on me by these happy people; I mean happy in their dispositions, in their apprehensions of rectitude with regard to our social or moral conduct: O divine simplicity and truth, friendship without fallacy or guile, hospitality disinterested, native, undefiled, unmodified by artificial refinements.
—William Bartram's impressions of the Cherokees at Watauga Town, 1775, Harper's

Watauga Town long vanquished, the ceremonial mound Bartram described is now a slight rise in a pasture behind the abandoned hull of Big D's convenience store. It would have been something to behold from horseback, riding north out of Nikwasee toward Cowee in 1775, miles of Cherokee corn and bean plantations spreading across the land and views of the high Nantahala and Cowee Mountains flanking his sides. This particular scene in *Travels* is intriguing, as it is one in which Bartram takes liberty to invite his readers to remove themselves from his unfolding narrative of the natural landscape and turn to the inner landscape that he also traverses and explores. Today, it is beheld through a windshield, punctuated by cold gray powerline pylons, flanked with odd billboards, real estate signs and advertisements for a diversity of nearby Protestant churches—both inner and outer landscapes under assault.

This significant Cherokee village was only a few miles up the road from where I live, but outside of the meager remains of the ceremonial mound and the aptly titled Watauga Creek, nothing is left to indicate its past presence. Sanderstown Road, Lyle Knob, Gibson Bottoms and Mason Mine are among the place names that link Anglo family histories and form the contents of the local geographic lexicon. Now the past rises up again in unforgettable and dramatic ways—Rebel flags flying from the backs of trucks as we arrive home, dotting the porches of Cowee and Watauga Towns, where those with no connection to the horror of the flag's meaning fly it with naïve rebellion. Land of my birth, land of my ancestors, land of the flag wavers whose kinfolk never owned slaves, who displaced a native people and did so in the name of the Lord.

My heart is still not right. I call my family doctor when we return and make an appointment. My EKG results in hand, he says calmly, "There is really nothing I can do for you. You should go to the ER. I can take you if your wife is not here." She is grocery shopping at the nearby Ingles, so he offers to go and find her with me, offering to take me if she isn't there.

After ICU and a procedure to correct the atrial fibrillation I have endured for eight days, my heart returns to normal, and I'm soon back to jogging and exercise. But my heart is no longer in this landscape as it once was. It's grown hardened against many of its human inhabitants who've had a good go at it, and there are many days I think I could leave. But this is my home, and I refuse. I stare into the giant red oak that has dominated this homeplace for unknown years. I've found remnants of Cherokee pottery beneath its heavy branches, and Bartram's path across the Cowee Mountains was nearby. Perhaps he passed by this tree when it was just a sprout. Rooted deeply to this place, its ancient presence anchors me, filling my heart with humility and respect.

Barry Lopez writes that the effort to know a place deeply is an expression of the human desire to belong and that the determination to know a place is consistently rewarded. What I appreciate is his insistence that every place is open to being known. And somewhere in this process, a person begins to sense that they themselves are becoming known, so that when they are absent from that place, they know that place misses them. And this reciprocity, to know and be known, reinforces a sense that one is necessary in the world. This idea carries me through the days when my wife and I feel so incredibly alone, when the only connection we feel is loyalty to the land and its non-upright inhabitants. It's then that I can feel the land's loyalty to us.

THE SABBATICAL

Record lows are occurring at my home in Cowee, North Carolina, with temperatures below zero, but I'm not there. I'm on a boat heading toward the Islas Ballestas off the coast of Paracas, Peru. I'm also on a three-month sabbatical from a nonprofit job, a conservation job that requires me to be so intimately and politically connected to the land and its inhabitants that I know of no other way to disconnect from it but to get as far away from it as I can afford to go. I know we're having record lows, as I'm following the weather every day on the Internet from this sunny, arid coast. And my neighbors e-mail me about it. One lets me know that water is flowing from under my house and onto the road. A river, he says. I find out that the owner of the vacation home next to my old farmhouse has come up from Florida for a visit and accidentally turned my water back on—after I had drained the pipes, winterized the place and escaped. She shares our well, an agreement I made with her after she bought the house, and has no idea as to the damage that this agreement is going to cost me.

The boat I am on is full of tourists. A cruise liner is parked across Pisco Bay from the dock where we are departing, and the passengers have all disembarked to take one of the many small boats that depart every two hours for the Islas. The cruise ship is a few miles away but is enormous in its scale and in its whiteness against the brick and ochre landscape. The scene is chaotic, seemingly disorganized, and it takes some time for the guides to get everyone into the dozen or so boats that are suddenly packed and roaring out to sea. We pass the Paracas Candelabra to our south, an enormous geoglyph

Sunset coastline of Paracas, Peru. *Photo by Angela Faye Martin.*

that dominates the northern face of Paracas peninsula of Pisco Bay, and our guide shouts out in Spanish a few of the more recent interpretations. Visible for twelve miles, it is believed to have been constructed around 200 BCE by the Paracas culture, which perhaps built it for nautical reasons or to symbolize the mythological lightning rod held by the pre-Inca and Inca god Viracocha, who rose from Lake Titicaca to create the moon, sun and stars. Viracocha, it was believed, would return during times of trouble. Or, as our guide says, it could symbolize the agricultural significance of the three principal crops of the Inca and pre-Inca: corn, potatoes and quinoa.

Regardless, it looms before us to the south, and today it symbolizes expensive vacations posted on Facebook. The smart phones are out and abundant, and I'm not sure if anyone is really listening. The boats plow on through the dark blue sea toward the Islas, growing larger by the minute. I'm not quite sure what to expect of this location described in places as the Peruvian Galapagos. I do expect something though, and something spectacular. It is also called the poor man's Galapagos, as the trips are affordable. The man seated behind me is drunk at 10:00 a.m. and is holding a Cusquena beer in his right hand while gripping the shoulder of a young boy of about thirteen years with his left. He is telling the boy how the islands were when he was here last, maybe twenty-five years ago. He is an American and boisterous, with a Mafioso style, and as I turn to study the Candelabra with my binoculars, I try not to make eye contact. I do want to listen though, as he is very excited about seeing the islands again, and for the boy to see them, who I begin to figure out is his nephew. Sea lions and more birds than you've ever seen before. *When I first came here, these boats didn't take you out like this; we went out on an old skiff with an Evinrude motor you started with a rope…*and on it goes for the entire trip.

The islands loom closer on the horizon, and we begin to see flocks of birds hovering by the thousands and inky spots dotting the rocky shores that soon emerge as sea lions. The boat becomes a polyglot of monosyllabic exclamations as four or five languages suddenly begin to focus on the spectacle ahead. The young guide becomes animated as we approach the first of the Islas on our journey, rattling off the species of birds that are crowded together among the blaring white guano: Inca terns, red legged cormorants, Peruvian boobies, Humboldt penguins and a half dozen species of gulls. The words roll off the tongue like a dream unfolding. Life in all its phantasmagoric diversity explodes before us, and I am taken by the gravity of the place, humbled, ashamed. Humbled because of the humility I should feel before all of creation, and ashamed, as the islands feel like a desperate refuge. Everything here is in exile because of human activities. I have never seen so many birds in one place.

The guide explains the increasing problems facing Humboldt penguins. The Humboldt Current is a cold, low-saline ocean current that flows north along the South American coast from southern Chile to northern Peru. It is one of the most productive marine ecosystems in the world, supporting one of the world's largest fisheries. It is also the reason why we are looking at a small cluster of endangered Humboldt penguins situated among a large flock of Peruvian boobies. Humboldt penguins are dependent on the cold-water fisheries of the current but are declining in numbers due to decades of exploitative fishing and guano harvesting and, now, climate change, along with habitat destruction by invasive species. The penguins are clearly overwhelmed here by the other species, which seem to fill every crevice of the windblown rocky crags. They sit atop one of the Isla's many pinnacles of rock, looking out of place and crowded. They look like what they are: a listed endangered species.

Not far from the penguins is a pair of red legged cormorants. This particular species of cormorant is non-colonial, unlike other cormorants and

Paracas National Park, Peru. *Photo by Angela Faye Martin.*

most seabirds. Their numbers are declining for many of the same reasons as Humboldt penguins, but they are not listed or protected as endangered—yet. The International Union for the Conservation of Nature (IUCN) lists them as near threatened. The one stunning pair we see out of the entire visit sits on a rock ledge about a foot wide, and we pass by within eight feet, where they seem unfazed and indifferent. Much like the penguins, they seem out of place—crowded, threatened. The guide is sympathetic. He turns the conversation toward threats—already mentioned—but most of these people are going to be back on the cruise ship in another few hours, and the others, like me, are going to be back in Paracas, sitting by a pool drinking Pisco Sours and staring out to sea.

I would love to be alone here for a while, but there is no such possibility. Except for scientists and the government-sanctioned guano harvesters, humans are not allowed on the islands. Guano harvesting is a major source of income for the handful of workers who are willing to risk life and limb every few years to gather an allotted amount from the rugged cliff sides. The tour guide explains that overharvesting from previous years is also a reason for bird population declines on the islands, though from where I gaze out there are birds in every crevice. The boats are giving one another a safe and comfortable distance, and for an hour, we bob among the roiling waves, churning within the islands' many inlets and passages as the guide points out various species, stopping when we turn a corner to find a large colony of sea lions scattered across one of the island's narrow beaches. The sea lions swim around the boat, and we are mesmerized. My wife points out to me that on shore an adult male has abducted a pup, a common behavior among single males without females, and the pup appears dead. The adult shakes the pup violently and throws it about, but our guide is not acknowledging it.

I don't think he is necessarily ignoring the scene, but it is a bit unsettling, this bit of raw nature that cuts against the grain of the experience. It would be awkward for him to point out, so as long as no one notices or raises a question, perhaps he thinks it best to keep floating toward the trip's conclusion, with the cameras snapping and everyone content. If we can ignore climate change, overfishing and the loss of species, surely we can ignore this. But this is visual. When people see this, they are upset. We don't see the other things, as they aren't in front of us or possible for us to touch. There's still plenty of food, gas, smart phones. Let's party. In the meantime, let me post this sea lion photo to Facebook.

THE MOUNTAINS WHERE I live are islands and rise above the valleys in places for more than six thousand feet. They are the highest mountains east of the Mississippi River. Once, there was only water here, goes the Cherokee creation story, and all of the animals lived in the sky realm. They grew tired of this and sent Water Beetle below the great ocean to bring forth mud to the surface and create land. Buzzard was sent to prepare the land for their arrival. He grew tired, and his wings pressed into the soft earth, creating this mountainous landscape where most of the animals still survive to this day. Many of these animals, as well as plants, are climate-dependent species that live nowhere else on earth. Some are leaving already and will likely be absent in the next fifty years. Fates seem to be sealed for many; others less so. Birds that can adapt and find new territories have a chance, for example, and creatures with more restricted habitats, such as salamanders, are in trouble. Audubon predicts that over two hundred species of birds in North Carolina are threatened by climate change, many of them perilously so.

The human animals who live in this landscape largely deny that this is happening and spend their time mostly preparing for other far less likely doomsday scenarios, such as economic collapse, terrorist Armageddon or various versions of the Second Coming. Record-low temperatures only mean that climate change and global warming are false theories and are proof that liberals and the international scientific community have conspired to help usher in one world government that will eventually seize their guns, ammo and oil-guzzling monster pickup trucks. I am not kidding; I hear this all the time. During the record cold here, one commentator in a local paper wrote in an attempt at humor, "Just think how cold this would be without global warming." It does not matter that within the last decade we have had record cold, record heat, record drought and record rainfall in western North Carolina—or that globally we have had one of the warmest years on record. Weird truly is the new normal, and the deniers are part of making it all the weirder.

When I return home from Peru a month later, I find my pipes shattered, and we have no running water. It is bitter cold, and after two days, we take our yet unpacked suitcases one county south to a remote mountain cabin my sister owns. We get eight inches of snow the first day there, the last day of February. Still reeling from the high summer climate and biodiversity of Peru, we take refuge in books and movies there for a month, slowly re-acclimating to the stark and empty winter woods, while contractors rip out and replace our plumbing, our laundry room and our kitchen. This is not the plan; the plan for the sabbatical was travel, lots of it—wilderness excursions into the Okefenokee Swamp and Cumberland Island, hiking the Bartram Trail, New Orleans. I tell myself this is not the sabbatical I want but it's the one that I get. I repeat often to myself a quote from Terry Tempest Williams: "Perhaps the most radical thing anyone can do today is stay home and attempt to still my mind and suppress the wanderlust." But I dream of Peru and the Islas Ballestas and wonder when the songbirds will return here from Central and South America, and every day I listen for them.

Viracocha brought life to land and Water Beetle brought land to life— wonderful inverse cosmologies of creation and existence. It was much more linear and far less interesting in the biblical Old Testament creation story: God created the world in six days, proclaimed it all good and then took a much-needed rest on the seventh. But this became the origin of the sabbatical concept, with the etymology of the term itself being derived from the Hebrew *Shabbat*, which literally means a ceasing, a rest—a long break every seventh year. The Israelites not only rested themselves but also rested the land every seven years—a land sabbatical. Over two thousand years later, I am heir to this concept—a concept placed into an abstract thing called a personnel policy that says I am eligible for this benefit every seven years. And I find no irony in the fact that the organization I am employed by works to ensure wild and special places receive a permanent rest from destructive human activities.

APRIL 14, 2015—THE LAST day of my sabbatical. For more than a week, the neotropical songbirds have been arriving. First, blue headed vireos, then parulas, followed within a day by black throated green, black and white and yellow throated warblers. And today a solitary hooded warbler. I was jogging in a light rain, and the forest was full of emergent greens and the territorial songs of these recent migrants. It was a slight break in otherwise heavy rains that we have been receiving for several days, with flash floods in many parts of our region, but the birds are oblivious, singing in what seems to be an ecstatic state as they mark off territories and seek mates. I'm growing tired of the rain but not as much as Peru. It's seen its heaviest rain there in eighty years—along with mudslides and fatalities. Parts of Peru are in a state of emergency. The director of Peru's Service of Meteorology and Hydrology attributes it to sea temperature increasing six degrees in the last few weeks, far above normal. All while California is turning into dust with record drought. The entire planet needs a sabbatical, I think, turning up the gravel road and running past the spot where the sawyer who built our home over one hundred years ago hauled most of this valley's timber to. And the birds continue to sing.

FISH, TRANSFORMATION AND
THINKING LIKE AN OSPREY

It is late February, and my wife and I are sitting in an ancient skiff a couple of miles off the coast of southeastern Costa Rica. From my view to the west, jungle meets ocean on both north and south sides of the grimy little surfer town of Puerto Viejo, where Gondoca Forest Reserve and Cahuita National Park serve as bookends, respectively. Puerto Viejo, where dreadlocked white American surfers patrol the streets when not out searching for the perfect wave, is our base for this area, where the natural and cultural worlds run together in a tapestry as thick as the Spanish mackerel schooling about our boat.

Our fishing guide, Earl, is one of the local Afro-Caribbean natives of the town who also owns the noisy and jumping late-night Neptune Bar. His assistant, a local Bribri Indian, speaks no English and can barely understand my faltering Spanish. When it is time to move on to the next location, he attacks the prehistoric Evinrude motor with a flurry of pulls and prayers. There are no life preservers, and the bottom is an inch deep with water, where our bait swims in dizzy and nervous circles, dodging our hands as we reach down to grab a fresh one for our hooks. Earl is smoking an enormous joint, drinking a cerveza Imperial and singing Bob Marley songs. It is maybe 9:00 a.m. He occasionally looks at us and tries to shove the joint our way. My wife looks at me cautiously. This is a look that she has mastered in our twelve-year marriage that is ignored to my certain peril.

She has also mastered the art of catching Spanish mackerel on this trip, and though she has caught the biggest fish for the day, she is far from being finished. She does not quit easily at this activity and does not easily let me win the biggest fish. Though she is motivated by competition when it comes to fishing, she is also motivated by a love of fish. She sees fish in so many ways—creatures that are sacred and to be appreciated for their unique role in our vast universe, creatures that can be caught for sport and released to grow or creatures that can feed us so we remain alive. Today, she decides we will keep the fish, cook them up with our guide and feed the volunteers at a local biomonitoring station.

The decision to keep fish is almost always hers to make, as fishing is something she commands when we are together. She seems to know the appropriateness and the when of keeping a fish, and I have learned not to question it. There doesn't seem to be anything mystical about these decisions, but there is a certain intuition she has about keeping fish to eat that I trust.

She also prides herself on her use of single hooks and criticizes me endlessly for the plugs I use that consist of a wicked array of double treble hooks. She considers it an unfair advantage on the fish, calls it a form of poaching and is shameless in her public persecution of me. On a recent trip to the Little Tennessee River near our home in Cowee, North Carolina, I hook a nice smallmouth bass of about two pounds, which I work through the shoals to the edge of our canoe, where I attempt to grab the fish by the lip. As I lift the fish into the boat, it makes a final surge of resistance, twisting the one dangling treble hook of my plug through the thin flesh along my right thumb. For several minutes, I am fish and man as I wrestle to free the fish with one hand while my wife watches from the bow of the boat.

I know what she is thinking, and she does not say it. Instead, she says, "Did you bring the needle nose pliers?" I stare at the blood dropping to the floor of the boat in slow rivulets. We are over an hour to the road by boat. No, I didn't. She paddles us to shore to stare at the large hook laced through the tight skin and sighs. I slowly begin a torturous task of cutting the hook from my thumb with a pocketknife. It is a stunning October day. Cardinal flower and Joe Pye weed at the apex of their expression provide backdrop as the blood flows and as this beautiful and righteous woman looks on with a mixture of concern and consternation. After a half hour of working the hook out, I take the paddle and begin our navigation back through the exquisite beauty of the river. We keep no fish.

Pale catfish glittering in moonlight. Silver bellied, thick whiskered. Throats slit, gut swept, drifting in a dark bucket. Warm-bottomed mud flats stinking of blood bait, rotten garbage, and motorboat flotsam. All the silent earth suspended in midnight's no tomorrow. Sleep moving in deep channels carving heartsong from summer sky.

Unlike most men I know, my earliest memories of fishing involve my mother. As a young divorcée in the Deep South, and a fundamentalist Christian, I suppose she was predisposed to a certain moral guilt that compelled her to plop a boy my age down in front of a farm pond with a cane pole and a box of pink worms. I'm sure it was something she considered critical to a proper southern boyhood. Or perhaps it was part of the larger family vision that the first-born grandson would go forth as a Fisher of Men, starting first with the real thing.

This is the beginning of her dream of normalcy: On hot summer Georgia afternoons, she loads her rattletrap blue Ford Maverick with me, my sister and a picnic lunch and drives us down to G.B.'s lake, where she pays for us to sit for hours as bobbers dance in the dark water and where our lack of skill occasionally intersects with luck, landing us an occasional bluegill or largemouth bass. And it is the beginning of my own rudimentary form of patience and contemplation as we sit in rickety lawn chairs and eat store-bought cheese crackers, drink Cokes and slap mosquitoes, smearing the bright-red blood across our thighs in streaks for kicks. We return home to our little brick house and fry fish afterward and sleep hard in the un–air conditioned and humid stillness.

The intersection of her dream and mine were not to occur.

Years later, as a teenager, fishing became representative of my independence. My mother remarried, and though the new family occasionally fled to Lake Allatoona for a weekend of camping and fishing, her two new stepdaughters took their toll on her time with us, as well as such previous frivolities as fishing. On spring and summer Saturdays, I would drive my old VW Beetle down to Sweetwater Creek, where I wade fished for rock bass, sleeping in the ruins of an old Civil War–era factory, dreaming of a life in the arctic wilderness where the fish ran thick and deep in endless miles of pristine emptiness.

Such dreams and realities of solitude were largely the result of fishing having also become an escape. The stepfather, a recovering alcoholic, slipped back into the monster of alcoholism following a car wreck, and home on the weekends was usually a place not to be. As a result, the hoped-for Fisher of Men became a hardened distruster of men and placed his faith in the forest and streams. There was a certain wisdom in this activity that I can appreciate now from my more comfortable midlife perspective. In Greco-Roman mythology, the fish held the symbolic meaning of change and transformation. Aphrodite and Hera both turned themselves into fish in order to escape the ferocious god Typhon, one of the most grotesque and hideous gods in all of Greek mythology.

And in ancient eastern Indian mythology, the fish is a symbol of transformation and creation. Vishnu transforms himself into a fish in order to save the world from a great flood. In the form of a fish, he guides King Manu's boat, which contained a few select survivors and seeds to replenish the world after its destruction.

This young man struggling with intense shyness and a less than desirable home life ran to the forest every chance he could in search of such transformation. Let me become fish, become forest. Let me drift within the feminine and flee Typhon's wrath in the swirling eddies of every river that has ever borne men away from such wrath. The fundamentalist salvation thrust upon me at such an early age certainly held no comparison to the baptism and rapture that the wild streams behind my home offered, so free of dogma and angry hands. This was a place instead that birthed miraculous passion that could sustain one far into the future, could keep one running toward the wild world and the fish that inhabit it forever.

Long ago, a decrepit stone foundation from a burned-out home stood within cutover pine woods. Water made its way there from a nearby spring. Fish made their way there. They drift motionless among the alder shadows in the thick summer heat. One is large and red-eyed and will not be fooled. The home is a vague memory. Southern African American children ran ponies there through the wild woods. Hogs lay in vast mud flats under the pine trees. When the fire came and burned the home, they were suddenly no more. White boys made their way there and then the men. Campfires burned at the pond's edge along the roots of an old beech tree, and a perfect quartz arrowhead lay in the dark soil by a stone spring box, waiting. One Saturday, an old drunk arrived in the late afternoon with a jackhammer and split the spillway and hauled off all the fish.

The boys stood slack jawed in fear of the man and stared at the large redeye bass they had sought for years. When the jackhammer stopped, the silence hummed like a bad guitar string. The fish are now gone, the foundation and mud flats covered with the monotonous drones of traffic and subdivisions. There is perhaps only one memory that remains of the place.

Down the road, a farm pond waits for me to come home so that I might serve my wife's ethics with a fly rod and a popping bug for bluegills. The Cowee range looms nearby, and a summer breeze blows down the valley, rattling the leaves on the large red oak next to our old farmhouse. The fish swirl in the murky pond water of my five-gallon bucket, and I clean each of them quickly under the pipe of an old artesian well that has pumped for decades from the depths of Cowee bedrock. I fry them on a propane stove under the oak's vast shadow and look through the window at my wife preparing the rest of our dinner in the warm August twilight.

Perhaps she is thinking that tomorrow will be a good day to go to the river. The river is low, and the fish are hemmed up in pools, hungry. She knows that we will see schools of redhorse working their way up the channels and the same pair of osprey that we see every year, traveling up and down the river together, fishing from the air and fleeing as we round each bend. The female darts along the edges of the river with her lifelong partner and swoops low as he dives into an eddy for something we cannot see. He emerges triumphant, and she cries her distinct, piercing cry. My wife says she is scolding him for keeping such a small fish.

TO KNOW A TREE

Space reaches from us and construes the world:
to know a tree, in its true element,
throw inner space around it, from that pure
abundance in you. Surround it with restraint.
It has no limits. Not till it is held
in your renouncing is it truly there.
—Rainer Maria Rilke, from "What Birds Plunge through
Is Not the Intimate Space"

The great northern red oak on this bright full-moon night is composed of snowfall and shadows, its labyrinth of contorted and time-altered branches alive with white and bursting with contrast against blue-black indigo sky. A few of its dead branches will likely split with weight tonight or tomorrow, and it will be a time to think twice about traversing beneath its looming presence. Some of these branches are a foot or more in diameter, and when they fall, the earth will split with their force and resonate with their impact. At its base, it is five feet across, and for twenty feet or more it rises with a slight taper before splitting into large two-foot limbs that depart in several directions upward, extending as long gnarly arms for thirty or more feet, dipping, rising, with other large branches breaking off in random and chaotic direction, and so on, until at the very end of this splitting there are only small twigs that signify the living, continued growing on.

Throughout winter, the only colors it has besides its intrinsic hues of gray and black are the whites of lichens and the greens of bryophytes and mistletoe. Of the bryophytes that cover its base and sides, the several I have been able to identify are poodle moss (*Anomodon attenuatus*), hook moss (*Leucodon andrewsiansus*), plait moss (*Hypnum pallescens*) and windswept broom moss (*Dicranum scoparium*). Clumps of mistletoe (*Phoradendron leucarpum*) protrude in its highest reaches, dark green and far beyond the possibility of shooting them down with a .22 rifle, as I do with other oaks up the ridge during the holiday season. No doubt other species line its branches, and could I fulfill my dream of climbing the tree, confirmation of this and other mysteries yet revealed would make my knowledge of it all the richer. In summer, its color is that of olive-colored leaves, and at the point where its main large bole breaks into branches, a moisture and detritus–filled depression occurs, where bright purple pokeweed and other small plants often grow, lording over their companions far below.

I have always admired old, large trees, yet it never occurred to me in my early years that someday I might find myself living so close to one. When I found myself exiting our car with a real estate agent and saw this tree, I knew this would soon be a reality. My wife and I were smitten by it and jokingly said that if the old farmhouse was too miserable, we would at least have the tree. I did not know at the time that this was not a joke at all and that the tree would soon have us. We bought the place and over twelve years later are still fighting to make the old home more livable, though surrendering more each day to the power of the tree. *Can a tree really have this type of power?* I ask, as I ponder our ability to continue on each winter, each election cycle, each weekend when we are alone with our tree and cultural and social connections are so far away.

A northern red oak (*Quercus rubra*) of this size could be anywhere between two and four hundred years old. If it's on the two hundred end of this period, it would have been a sapling in the early nineteenth century, having sprouted sometime during the Cherokee removal and left to grow for some reason, while every other tree in this valley was cut and sawed during the next one hundred years. The house itself adds a bit to the mystery of the tree. It was built sometime in the late nineteenth century, and what was here before it is unknown. Beneath the front door is a large stacked pile of stones approximately five feet wide by five feet high. There is no reason for such a pile of stones, unless there was once a chimney in this location. One woman in her nineties who grew up in the house has come by a few times and reminisced about the interior and helped us understand the layout of

Northern red oak in winter with author's home in background. *Photo by Angela Faye Martin.*

the home, but the current fireplace location and interior was exactly now as it was when she was a child. Many of the settlers who moved here following Cherokee removal took over Cherokee homes and farms, so there could have been a Cherokee dwelling here at one point. Cherokee pottery shards we have found in our garden indicate this possibility. And she remembers the tree being as large then as it is now. This suggests that it could have been an important tree to a previous owner.

Regardless, with the exception of a small stand of various oak species far up the ridge in a rock-strewn boulder field behind our house, this tree has been here much, much longer than any other tree that grows in Cowee valley today. In its immediate vicinity and for a quarter mile in any direction, the trees are for the most part between twenty and fifty years old. Farther up the mountain on to the national forest, they are even younger, having been cut in the recent decade, or older, somewhere between seventy and one hundred years old, recovering after the industrial logging of the early twentieth century. What gave this one old oak the power to stay on, what memories does it contain and what feelings does it share with the surrounding forest? Is the melancholy it exudes the result of bearing witness to so much death and destruction?

The ancient Greeks and Romans worshiped oaks, and evidence suggests that this reverence was shared by many branches of European Aryan stock (an accepted anthropological term but nonetheless what birthed modern-day skinheads and bizarre racist ideology). Sir James Frazer, in the classic *The Golden Bough*, goes into this in depth. Zeus and Jupiter, highest gods of both Greek and Roman mythology and divinities of the sky, rain and thunder, were revered as the spirit of the oak. Zeus was also considered the bearer of lightning, as oaks were struck more often by lightning than other trees. Areas where oaks were struck by lightning were also considered sacred, often being fenced in for their protection. The Druids chose groves of oaks for their sacred services and considered nothing more sacred than the mistletoe, which grew almost exclusively on oaks. Ancient Germans, Slavs and Lithuanians all considered oaks sacred trees, and sacrifices to oaks were common for fertility, good crops and rain. Mistletoe was considered to contain the life and essence of the sacred tree and was known as the Golden Bough throughout Britain and other parts of Europe for its mystical qualities. According to Frazer, this was likely due to the fact that mistletoe remained green throughout winter while the oak was leafless and that it turns a bright golden color when dried. Mistletoe was used to ward off witchcraft or guard a soldier in battle, placed in cribs to ward off elves and placed under a pillow on Midsummer Eve to induce prophetic dreams. Its use as an aphrodisiac and fertility enhancer dates back to the ancient Greek festivals of Saturnalia, the origins of the most common American use of it during the Christmas season, when it is placed beneath doorways for couples to meet and kiss.

When inability to sleep drives me to rise on nights like this and look out the window, the tree's presence is the first thing I am conscious of. I feel and like to believe that the tree is conscious of me and lean on this belief often while I am outside working, pruning or cutting firewood. I sometimes find it hard to believe otherwise, though I do challenge myself to do so. Yet from where does this feeling arise when I am cutting locusts and mimosa, and the occasional walnut, that grow quick and high from the bank next to my garden and well-tended mountain camellias and *Franklinia*? I have actually caught myself with apologetic feelings and guilt as I work, with the oak looming above, seemingly glaring, and with me hoping that it understands the mission of my endeavors, my hope that it knows that I would never dare cut one branch from its mighty being. This effort to understand communication within the plant world is nothing new. German forest ranger Peter Wohlleben, in *The Hidden Life of Trees*, documents decades of his and other scientific researchers' work revealing how forest trees are social beings, with the ability to learn and remember, nurse their young and old and warn each other of dangers through fungal networks. The German tradition of attention to trees and silviculture is legendary, in both the arts and the sciences, and upon reading Wohlleben's observations, my mind immediately turns to the early twentieth-century German poet Rainer Maria Rilke. Rilke wrote mystically about the power of trees, with observations that seem to now translate into science: these trees are magnificent, but even more magnificent is the sublime and moving space between them, as though with their growth it, too, increased. Maybe it's just me, but this sounds a lot like consciousness observed within the plant world.

If I look out from any window or door, I see empty homes. There are five altogether, and were I able to look farther up the ridge or through the woods, I would see more. Vacation homes all, which only contain visitors a few times a year. From the rear of our house, a small cabin owned by an English couple lies dormant from November until May, when they arrive eagerly with power tools, lawnmower, herbicides and leaf blowers to attack the place with proper British vigor, intent on sprucing it up before spending one or two nights there. The home is tucked up into the small cove behind us, surrounded by tulip trees and a few small-diameter white oaks. The tulip trees are young, maybe thirty or forty years old, but the couple is concerned that they will blow over in a storm. It's unlikely, but they talk about it fairly often, so I'm sure they will soon have them cut. A large and stately white oak that was of a strength I cannot imagine, and which supplied us with firewood for a winter, was recently cut by them. Theirs is a suburban lawn perspective, and they likely fear that our anarchic approach to wild gardening and reverence for the renegade trees around our home will eventually result in damage. The oak stands like a sentinel among this array of homes, and when we observe it from afar while walking our gravel lane home from the mailboxes a quarter mile down the road, it dominates all.

To our east, an old green house sits back in the woods, slowly being overtaken by English ivy, the ivy already covering several large white oaks that have grown up next to it. Over almost a decade, I saw a light on in it on one occasion. A couple bought it on the Internet during the real estate boom here and lost interest quickly, and following the crash, it was soon in bank ownership. It was abandoned for several years until a fun and high-spirited gay couple from Florida bought it and came up a few times and piddled with it, but they have not been back in a long time. We had hopes that they would make something of it, as we enjoyed their company greatly, but I think it will be on the market again soon. The meadow that separates us from it is growing back in lanky mimosas and spindly walnuts and a few buckeyes. The mimosa appears to be winning, as they always do here, but shadowing them all are the enormous arms of the red oak. They will not do well in its massive shadow, as they need all of the sunlight they can get.

Directly to our north, and too close for comfort, is a small vacation home owned by a retired couple from Charlotte. This is one of their three houses, with it being primarily a summer home, though they do come up on occasion to experience snowfall when we get it in any significance. Their knowledge of the area is nil, as is that of all the vacation home owners, but they come over and putz about beneath our giant oak and feign knowledge and interest in our mountain camellias and strange and gangly *Franklinias*. The tree upon its first encounter always gains comment, though large trees where they come from are likely more common. An observation I make in cities often is that large trees are more abundant since they have grown undisturbed in yards or parks for decades and in flood plain ravines where development isn't possible, and they have been left alone to grow.

On the ridge just above our house to the south, two small vacation homes sit empty on winter nights. I have never met the owners of one, but the other is owned by two thirty-something married professionals who live near Athens, Georgia. A chemist and a pharmacist, they come up on the weekends during the warmer months, and occasionally in the winter, to mountain bike, paddle and hike, often stopping by to say hello and observe us like creatures in a zoo. During the summer months, the oak is so full of greenery that it blocks their view of us, whereas in the winter months they are able to see through its large branches directly into our sitting room and kitchen. We have only talked of the tree with them once, while lunching in their dining room looking down through it to our rusted metal roof and weedy garden.

Yet the tree is the centerpiece for this odd slice of landscape, tucked up in this small mountain hollow where it has touched down like Pegasus, where I cannot help but imagine its dark sense of humor as it watches this brief unfolding of comings and goings, forcing me to ponder my own existence and sense of time. It knows no other place, can go no other place. This is its place, the only place it will ever know. Observing all surrounding it through powers I cannot know or understand, it absorbs all, a repository of unknown observations, a witness to events I can only dream about. There have been times when it seemed like a giant receptor, an antenna wavering about among its dwarfed brethren below, as strong winds blew and the earth's signals crashed into its branches. That this is not too far-out of an idea is comforting. Researcher Dave Milarch, author of *The Man Who Planted Trees*, has defined trees as solar collectors of cosmic radiation and writes that energies inside the earth are transmuted and transmitted into the cosmos by them, saying that "trees are like antennas, sender and receivers of earth energies and stellar energies." He and other researchers have shown that billions of stars influence the earth with their radiation and that cosmic radiation impacts tree growth even more than annual temperature or rainfall. One of these researchers, Lawrence Edwards, has shown that tree buds change shape and size rhythmically, in regular cycles through winter, directly correlating to the moon and planets. Oaks such as this one appear to change with Mars. I don't know where Mars is tonight, or if it is even visible, but if I could see this tree's buds changing shape and size right now, I am afraid its power might bring me to my knees.

There is a local story about another enormous tree in Cowee valley, one that reportedly was cut in the 1940s. Known as the Fed Raby poplar, after a fugitive by that name, this tree was so large that Fed hid out in it comfortably for several years. The account of the man and the tree was published in a Cashiers, North Carolina historical journal and passed on to me by a friend. According to the story, Fed murdered someone at dance in Polk County, North Carolina, under questionable circumstances, and was branded with

Northern red oak in summer with author's home in background. *Photo by Angela Faye Martin.*

the letter *M* on his forehead and released. The *M* would allow anyone to kill him without retribution. This was in the late nineteenth century, and the forests here were yet largely uncut. Fed fled to this area, crossing the dense spruce forests of the Balsam range, then the Cowee Mountains, into Bee Branch cove in Cowee valley. Locals who remembered him at the time of the story's recording said that he built a crude sleeping loft with a ladder in the ten-foot-diameter poplar (*Liriodendron tulipifera*). When the tree was felled, the lumbermen used nine-foot crosscut saws, and the tree was so large that it had to be quartered to be loaded onto a logging truck. A woman interviewed in the story who remembered the tree said that a ten-foot plank could be turned around inside the tree. Regardless of the truth of that statement, that a man could build a loft inside it and live is nonetheless remarkable.

In nearby Tellico valley, one of the largest white oaks (*Quercus alba*) in the state still lives. White oaks can live for six hundred years, and though the tree is likely a state champion, it is not listed in the champion tree list for North Carolina. It is over eight feet across, with an enormous crown spread, sitting among large rocks in a well-manicured, stone-walled enclosure dating back to the nineteenth century. Tellico was a Cherokee village site prior to their removal in 1838, and the tree served as a central meeting place for the inhabitants. I take anyone who visits my home and has the interest to see this tree. I have seen no other like it. Much like our red oak, it has a haunting and consuming presence. Standing close to it and centering yourself in its being will remove you from your present-day constraints. Awe is the most common human reaction. I revere it and desire its patience.

But for the large sycamores that grow along the nearby Little Tennessee River, this is it for the large trees in my secluded north Macon County valley of Cowee. I have explored most of the mountain ranges in this valley with an employee of our State Natural Heritage Program, and though we found small pockets of miraculously spared old-growth forest, none of the trees was of the size of the old oak that sits a few yards out my window from where I write. The valley was once full of them though, and many other species of this size. American chestnuts, tulip trees and numerous species of oaks with these dimensions all grew plentiful. Large oaks still dot the larger landscape of the Little Tennessee Valley, always around homesites, where the residents keep them for shade and beauty, and perhaps for unconscious reasons that date back to their Celtic and Aryan ancestors, some genetic hardwiring that says keep this one, fire and power are contained here, mystery resides within. I'm going with the unconscious reasons, as mystery and magic seem in short supply these days, and I'm going to hedge a bet that something larger is going on, something we will learn more of as scientists uncover more of the hidden life of trees. Photo historian John Wood has said of photographer Beth Moon's stunning images of ancient trees that such photos "can lead us to considerations of the most compelling issue of our age, the reenchantment of the world." That is why I am staring into this tree's stark branches tonight—my own compulsion to be enchanted and reenchanted with the world.

THREE FORKS

At Three Forks, the Left Fork of Raven Fork seems relatively gentle and benign, but by the time it gets there it has descended through some of the most forbidding wilderness in the eastern United States from its source under Tricorner Knob, on the backbone of the Smokies.
—Ted Alexander, timber cruiser and fishing guide, from his 1920s account of working in the Raven's Fork watershed, Mountain Fever

I had never seen a handheld GPS unit go haywire, but there it was, cradled within my friend Hugh Irwin's cold and shaking palm, making no sense as we stood in pouring rain and lightning somewhere along a spine of mountain aptly titled Breakneck Ridge. We had left that morning out of Three Forks, a wild area of virgin spruce forest deep within the eastern half of the Great Smoky Mountains National Park, where we had spent the last two nights in what many consider one of the most pristine and remote places left in southern Appalachia. Though overnight camping is not allowed in this area, the park service granted us permission due to Hugh's reputation and credentials as a forest ecologist, along with his interest in documenting the area's old-growth characteristics. Becoming more anxious and hypothermic by the moment, we at last found the small saddle of land that would take us over to Hyatt Ridge, where we could walk our remaining soggy miles out on a somewhat established trail.

Perched within a high-elevation valley and cut off from the more established visitor locations and trails by a rugged and narrow gorge,

Three Forks is a hydrological and forested wonder. Its name derives from the fact that three streams come together at a shared terminus, forming a long, deep pool and the beginning of Raven Fork, one of many large and iconic streams that characterize the Great Smokies. Though Native Americans likely accessed Three Forks for thousands of years, the first documented exploration of the area began in 1799, when crews surveying the Tennessee–North Carolina state line attempted to enter it, only to abandon their efforts after becoming entangled in the dense rhododendron, spruce and fir. Another failed attempt occurred in 1821, and it was not until 1858, when Swiss-born geographer Arnold Guyot explored the area, that some accuracy was provided as to the location of the state line. But as Ravensford timber cruiser Ted Alexander noted while exploring the area in the 1920s, even Guyot made mistakes mapping the Smokies main range in the area, as did subsequent U.S. Geological Survey attempts.

Much like the survey crew of 1799, my first attempt to enter Three Forks failed for the same exact reasons. My wife and I had camped with Hugh at McGee Springs, thinking we would bushwhack out Breakneck Ridge and descend along the old manway that Ted Alexander forged almost eighty years earlier when creating a fishing camp at Three Forks. Unable to find even a remnant of this path, we retreated after hours of entanglement in dense rhododendron and ancient fallen spruce and hemlock. At one point, Hugh's pack was unknowingly unzipped by a rhododendron snag, spilling his GPS unit into the thickly vegetated forest floor. Upon realizing this a half hour later, we backtracked on hands and knees for close to two hours, scouring the ground until at last we saw an alien glint of metal within the thick carpet of green. Beaten, bruised, but undeterred, we decided that night around our campfire at McGee that we would return with more determination and preparation for our next attempt.

When we finally made it to Three Forks on our second attempt, I had felt a sense of timelessness like I had never experienced before—the forest primeval, untouched by senseless modern human hands. It is fairy tale–like in its appearance, Jurassic in its feel. We had found a bit of the old manway, hacked out in the 1920s by Tom Alexander and George Masa, and had crawled, slid and prayed our way down it over several hours, wondering all along how we were going to turn around and crawl our way back out after making our destination, since we had again decided to camp at McGee Springs and day-trip the excursion. At last reaching the great confluence of the three streams, we enjoyed a brisk swim and brief exploration of the area before making the brutal climb out and returning to camp.

On our second successful trip into Three Forks, Hugh obtained permission for us to overnight. Fires are forbidden, so that first evening, we huddled quietly around candlelight, listening to wood thrush in the crepuscular light, the only sound we heard but for the continuous babble of Raven Fork. Hugh and another friend who was along, Rob Cox, were to set out and explore the watershed the next day. With no trails, and a topographic map as their only guide, it would be a challenge. The only early descriptions we have of the area are from Tom Alexander's journals, and these are almost a century old. Alexander explored the area as a timber cruiser in the 1920s for the James D. Lacey Company and its client Ravensford Lumber Company, tallying the commercial value of the ancient forest prior to its sale to the Department of Interior and the establishment of the Great Smoky Mountains National Park. Ravensford owned thirty-five thousand acres in the high elevation basin, and Alexander fell in love with it, so when the Lacey Company went broke in 1929, owing him $600 in back salary, he quickly seized upon the opportunity by negotiating the use of the camp at Three Forks and all of its gear as a settlement.

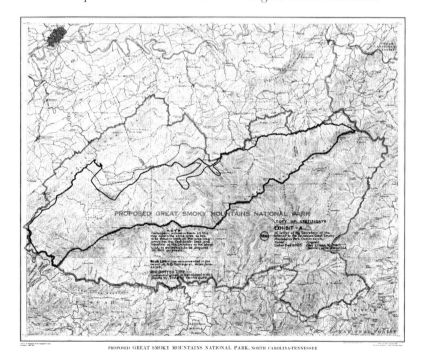

Map of proposed Great Smoky Mountains National Park, 1929. *Tennessee State Library and Archives.*

Alexander referred to Three Forks as one of the "finest trout streams in the southern Appalachians even if only the most dedicated fishermen could actually get to it." He quickly established a tourist fishing camp there, hiring a cook and declaring that if fishermen "had any trout fishing skill at all, we could practically guarantee them all the fish they wanted." Almost one hundred years later, I have fished these waters and caught between forty and fifty brook trout a day with little effort. There was an old hunters' cabin at Three Forks at the time of Alexander's explorations, and he soon added a few canvas wall tents and a cook shed to accommodate his many visitors willing to make the rugged nine-mile walk in from Smokemont.

One of these was Japanese photographer George Masa, who became close friends with Alexander, traveling to Three Forks to photograph the stunning beauty of the area. Like all great photographers, Masa captured the spirit of the place, and I refer to his images in Alexander's book often when conjuring up my own memories. Masa photographed Alexander's fishing camp often, and in one of his last photographs taken in 1931, there is a large group of Asheville men and women huddled around a campfire with Masa's famous converted bicycle measuring wheel leaning against a tent pole. The camp is large and hospitable in appearance, and camp cook Avery Gouge stands in a professional-looking apron with buttoned-up collared shirt.

Masa was also close friends with Horace Kephart and worked alongside him in his efforts to build support for the Great Smoky Mountains National Park. Masa died of influenza in Asheville in 1933, destitute, with an unfulfilled burial wish to be buried next to Kephart in Bryson City.

There are no remains of Alexander's camp left today, though someone did make it in at some point with some large sheets of plastic tarp that lay rolled on the ground in a miserable state of decay. Unless we can pack it out, this ugly desecration will likely be here for one hundred years before vanishing from human sight. There is also an old wooden picnic table made from rough-cut logs and lashed to two stout young spruce trees. Hugh thinks he knows the origins of the trash and table and explains:

After I moved to Asheville, [my wife] Janice and I did a hike with David and Kim Thompson and camped at the Backcountry site where the Enloe Creek Trail crosses Raven Fork Creek. This was my first time to see Raven Fork Creek, and I was impressed by how beautiful and wild it is. I knew that the Harvey Broome Group (a local Sierra Club chapter) had come downstream here and had read that there used to be an old trail coming down beside the creek. There were two guys fishing the creek in the vicinity of the camp. We knew they were there when we saw two backpacks stowed under a boulder near the camp. Later in the day, we ran into them fishing in the stream. One guy was a local who lived in the Cherokee area and was very talkative (too much so). The other guy didn't say anything and avoided us. The talkative guy said they had caught over one hundred trout that day; most they had released, but they were planning on cooking some. When we got back to camp, the talkative guy proceeded to retrieve all kinds of equipment he had stashed nearby—a pan and Crisco was stored in a hollow tree. He had a saw and talked about an axe he had under a rock nearby. He said he came to the area a lot and kept this stuff there to use when he was there.

The other guy kept to himself and kept his face in the shadows, but he was fairly close since the campsite is tiny. He was supposedly the talkative guy's cousin from Tennessee. There were extremely weird vibes going on. The guy talked about the Park Service picking up garbage in the backcountry, and the next morning when we got up, there was a big garbage bag of trash hung in the bear bag pulleys for the site—we carried it out. The guys were gone. They had apparently hiked out after we went to bed; they had actually talked about their intention to do this. This was when Eric Rudolph was at large. We saw a photo of him shortly after this. Janice is convinced that the reclusive guy was Rudolph, and I'm more than half convinced myself it was him. Hey, fugitives need vacations too. I do think that some of the camp remains—tarps, trash, nails and structures built in trees—are left by the talkative guy. It's his style, and I'm pretty sure he gets up in the Three Forks area—in fact, he referred to this while he was talking.

I can easily imagine Rudolph staying hidden out in here without much worry of being detected. That he was found dumpster diving in Murphy does not say much for his backcountry skills though, but he no doubt hid out within these wildest of places for years before the most expensive and exhaustive manhunt in U.S. history ended with him being retrieved from a dumpster.

A WEEK AFTER HUGH and I survive the storm and confusion of this fourth and most recent trip, Lamar Marshall, a friend who is documenting ancient Cherokee trails and trade routes, traveled to Three Forks with three

Cherokees to see the magnificence and experience the sacredness of the place. When I ask him how the trip was, he writes back to say that it was one of the toughest days he had ever spent in the woods. This is quite a statement coming from someone who has spent more time in the woods than probably anyone I know. They had ridden horses to McGee Springs and then started out looking for the manway on Breakneck Ridge. They had found old survey tape and then "crawled, slid, and descended for 2.6 miles" to the confluence of the three streams. They all swam there, and the Cherokees told Lamar that to do so was good medicine. They then attempted to go up McGee Springs, thinking that it could be no worse than the "trail" they had attempted on the way down. This route was also to be over a mile shorter and more direct to McGee Springs where the horses waited. On their way up, Lamar tells me, one of the strangest things that has ever happened to him occurred. It is worth quoting at length.

I can summarize to say it was one of the toughest days in the woods of my life. Gil Jackson is a helluva 58-year-old Cherokee. He had his two Cherokee acquaintances who live way back in the Qualla Boundary past Big Witch Road to load their horses and we three drove to Round Bottom. Rode horses to McGee Springs, cross-tied the horses to trees. Found the faint trace with sparce ribbons on it and started over Breakneck. I was GPSing the way. That trail was the absolute worst I have ever slid, crawled and descended. It was 2.6 miles to Three Forks. I knew I was in trouble to have to walk that trail back out. We all swam in the pool which was at least 7 feet deep and a real gonad freezer. It was 3:30 by then and we decided that it would be easier to walk Raven Fork upstream and find where McGee Spring Creek joined Raven and we would go up there. As the crow flies, GPS said 1.4 miles and it was fairly a straight shot up the creek. We waded up Raven about ¼ mile slipping and sliding, climbing through and around giant log jams in the laurel, and the only reservation I had was going up Breakneck if we hit laurel as bad as on the trail in, except with no trail at all.

About this time the strangest thing that ever happened to me happened. I slipped and fell into a small pool that was only 3 feet across and about 3 feet deep, and about 6 feet long. The water fell into the pool upstream only a few feet and went out a small chute right where I slipped. My left hand with my GPS in it went under water and it felt like somebody snatched my GPS out of my hand and it disappeared. I watched to see if it would pop up and go over the little chute—I never saw it. I fished in the rocks underwater to see if it was trapped. The three Cherokees went back downstream for several hundred yards to see if it had floated down. We looked and looked and I realized it was gone forever. All I had was my compass and a very old crummy Smokies map with a scale of 1 mile per inch. I got a rough compass bearing to McGee Springs and drew a course on the map and it was now after 4:00. We still had to climb Breakneck and were getting worried now about getting out before dark.

We continued wading up Raven looking for Rapid Creek to enter on left. Finally found that. Gil took two bad falls on the slick rocks and I monkey crawled as I did not want to bust a knee. I slipped once and slid on my pack down into a pool but as I was already soaked what the hell. At 5:30 we found McGee Spring and a flag where somebody marked the confluence. We went up and there was no laurel but thick umbrella plants. Tough with boot fulls of water. Tough keeping up with any one of them as they have been running the mountains all their life. Only Gil had been to Three Forks before. We lost the spring somewhere up the mountain and angled off to the south to keep from missing McGee too far east where we would really be good and lost and we intersected the trail a quarter mile or so north of McGee Spring. Got lost near where Breakneck drops into the saddle of McGee Springs and circled until nearly dark. It was looking grim. I was about to pull the old space blanket out and build a fire when Gil found the trace and we found the horses and rode out at last light. Riding down those narrow trails at dusk with the night birds sounding off on horses almost gave me the eerie feeling that I had traveled back in time and would soon smell the 100 campfires of the village as we gained the bottom. It also left me with an eerie feeling that the Little People or some other Cherokee force snatched my electronic device attuned to government satellites out of my hand and told us to go out according to the Old Ways.

One of the Cherokees knew many plants along the trail, most by other names and what could be ate and used for medicine, learned from his grandpa who was long gone. One was called bean plant. We ate it and it did taste like green beans. This guy killed 18 deer last year and several hogs. Hunts with a bow, a crossbow, a muzzle loader and modern rifle.

I'm a little sore today but not too bad. Gil says special thanks to Hugh and Brent and whoever else toted the plastic out of Three Forks. It is a special place to the Cherokees.

Walking out now on weak and wobbling legs, with torn clothing and pack sagging with water and ancient trash, I am wondering if I will ever return.

It is my third "successful" trip into Three Forks, and I am pretty sure I have asked myself this upon every leaving. Hopefully the memory of this tortuous exit will soften and the memories of catching wild brook trout all day long, drinking wine while several of them simmer on our small gas stove and the crepuscular wood thrush singing the evening in will win out and I'll be back before I'm too old to even consider it. But if I don't, I'll take pleasure in knowing that it's there.

MODERN APPALACHIA AND

THE DEATH OF THE SUBLIME

The passion caused by the great and sublime in nature, when those causes operate most powerful is astonishment; and astonishment is that state of the soul in which all its motions are suspended, with some degree of horror. In this case the mind is so entirely filled with its object, that it cannot entertain any other, nor by consequence reason on that object which employs it. Hence arises the great power of the sublime, that, far from being produced by them, it anticipates our reasonings, and hurries us on by an irresistible force. Astonishment, as I have said, is the effect of the sublime in its highest degree; the inferior effects are admiration, reverence, and respect.
—Edmund Burke

Jewelweed shakes in the late September breeze, pale and wavering within the electric red wands of cardinal flower. Dark purple stems of pokeweed, heavy with seed, bend in arcs of contrast against the many fading greens, while ruby-throated hummingbirds flit through the afternoon light—all of this contained in my narrow field of vision from beneath the lemon yellow of fading catalpa leaves. Bucolic Cowee valley seems under the spell of shifting autumn light, and the words that come to mind for this moment, or at least for the desire of this moment, are transcendent and sublime—words that arise from imagination and history, anachronistic today, but adequate and relevant to the desires of my cynical and overwrought twenty-first-century consciousness. It wasn't always this way. The eighteenth-century British statesman Sir Edmund Burke spent a good part of his life pondering the word *sublime* in an attempt to understand the human range of senses and emotions and to create a proper response to what he and others considered to be the intellectual staleness of the Enlightenment. Burke's 1757 *A Philosophical Inquiry into the Sublime and Beautiful* helped usher in the Romantic movement, with its emphasis on emotional truth and its attempt to understand nature through art, literature and religion. Arriving here in western North Carolina's Cowee valley in May 1775 was the first eighteenth-century American to immerse himself in these ideas: the writer, artist, naturalist and horticulturalist William Bartram.

Bartram traveled to Cowee valley in May of that year on the eve of the American Revolution, alone and on the prowl for plant specimens to ship to his English patron, John Fothergill. Based on his 1791 publication, *Travels*, the word *sublime* was on his mind quite a bit. When he entered Cowee valley, capital of the Middle Town Cherokees and site of my old mountain home, he saw the mountains with "grandeur and sublimity" and the valley itself as situated "amidst sublimely high forests." When he reached the crest of the nearby Nantahala Mountains, he "beheld with rapture and astonishment, a sublimely awful scene of power and magnificence, a world of mountains piled upon mountains." The historian Roderick Nash, author of *Wilderness and the American Mind*, credits Bartram with introducing the word into American literature and being one of the first Americans to describe the American landscape in such terms. This was contrary to the settler zeitgeist, which saw the American Wilderness as a place to be conquered and subdued, along with its native inhabitants.

Cowee would be brutally destroyed the following year, and the settlers would soon pour in, their ancestors today now hanging on to remnants of the large parcels that many of them acquired for nothing or next to nothing. The once capital of the Middle Town Cherokees is but a ghost of itself now, though its ceremonial mound is now permanently conserved and back in tribal ownership after two hundred years. But the ghost is a powerful one. Cherokee place names dot the landscape, along with ethnobotanical and cultural artifacts. Except for the mound and the roadside historical marker, there is no other visual reference. Our most valuable descriptions of Cowee prior to this can be accredited to Bartram, as well as his descriptions of the Appalachian plant world, theretofore unknown to science. He was only here for a couple of weeks, but he nonetheless devoted a significant portion of *Travels* to this period. He describes Cowee as "one of the most charming mountain landscapes perhaps anywhere to be seen," and his time spent with the Cherokees is one of compassionate cultural observation and a

Artwork by William Bartram. *Courtesy of Natural History Museum, London.*

unique sensitivity to their customs and traditions. I once heard the Cherokee scholar and language expert Thom Belt present a possible Native American perspective on Bartram's time spent among them here in Cowee. To Belt, Bartram was the first white man to come among them who didn't have a gun, a Bible, something to trade or papers for them to sign. He was simply curious and open to knowing them and the natural world they inhabited.

When Bartram arrived in the Cherokee town of Watauga, several miles upriver from Cowee, he was greeted by the chief, whom Bartram describes as a man "universally beloved" and "revered by all for his exemplary virtues." He describes his time there as one of "perfect and agreeable hospitality" and bestows the highest compliments upon the people for their happiness— undefiled and unmodified by artificial refinements. "O Divine simplicity and truth, friendship without fallacy or guile"—this was his emphatic reaction to this brief visit and a subtle criticism of what he considered to be the utter lack of such values in eighteenth-century society. Subsequently, *Travels* was criticized by American critics upon its publication in 1791 and nowhere near so well received as it was with its European counterparts. America was still full of revolutionary pride and still in the throes of Native American conquest across the country. Bartram's argument for the shared humanity of those southern tribes like the Cherokee was unpopular, and even after the Cherokees adopted Christianity and western ways, they were still brutally removed and their property stolen. The heirs of this legacy surround me here in far western North Carolina today, where anti–federal government sentiments of all sorts reside, along with resistance to local government regulations, planning and outside influence of any kind.

Much like the trade paths that crisscrossed the mountains here at the time of Bartram's visit, *Travels* was a major intellectual intersection of sorts. Scientific in its Linnaean nomenclature and romantic in its effusive emotional response to the landscape and people he encountered, it reveals Bartram's struggle to integrate the two into a coherent rendering that captures the best of the Enlightenment era and the beginning of the Romantic. But what strikes me most about his reaction to the people and landscape of these mountains is his humility. This was not a popular emotion at the time, when thoughts of revolution, conquest and subjugation were on the general public's mind, but if there is one word that perhaps captures the spirit of his writings, humility is it. It can also be argued that it was the beginning of an American natural history tradition. Historian Phillip Marshall Hicks says in *The Development of the Natural History Essay in American Literature* that Bartram was "the first genuine and artistic interpretation of the American landscape" and that "*Travels* was the first combination of accurate observation, aesthetic appreciation and philosophical interest in the realm of natural history literature." Bartram's humble approach to humanity and nature would take hold among a core group of American and British writers in the late eighteenth and early nineteenth centuries with the Romantic movement, which laid the foundation for what was to become one of the core principles of the late nineteenth- and early twentieth-century conservation movement. It might be a stretch, but given the impact of *Travels* on the development of the Romantic movement and the fact that it was rooted in the southern landscape, it can be claimed as another piece of the southern influence on American literature.

Bartram's sympathetic views of Native Americans and artistic treatment of the American South were highly influential with the early nineteenth-century English Romantic writers Samuel Taylor Coleridge and William Wordsworth, who borrowed heavily from his imagery and who, in turn, influenced early American Romantics such as Henry David Thoreau and

Artwork by William Bartram. *Courtesy of Natural History Museum, London.*

Ralph Waldo Emerson. This link is often ignored in the history of America's Romantic movement, but it's a clear one and significant. America at this time was industrializing in the Northeast, conquering the West, converting my native Southeast to slave-based agriculture and cutting down the forests here with unbridled rapaciousness. The subsequent effect of this in the coming decades was a national call for the conservation of our last wild places, along with the further divide between those who would as soon continue exploiting them. It was also the beginning of divisions in America between rural and urban perspectives with regard to the land. Urban and industrial America called for conservation and preservation, while rural Americans, as well as corporate America, saw the vast expanse of publicly owned land as either a commons to be utilized or as a natural resource base to be exploited for profit. This early national divide is a significant piece of what would later become the more multifaceted political divide of what we now call red and blue places.

Here today in the deep politically red country of Cowee, Bartram's legacy is mostly unknown, and were it not for a trail given his name and the efforts of a few local writers and organizations, it would go largely unnoticed. Yet his legacy is profound for those of us who spend time with his writings, puzzling over his routes and creating a palimpsest from his details and descriptions. It adds wonder to the place, as well as an important historical dimension. I need this wonder, as I once held Appalachia on a pedestal, a place in my young imagination where the people and customs documented in the voluminous Foxfire series represented a type of freedom and way of life that I admired and longed for. These youthful romantic notions led me here eventually, where I pursued a career of conservation and sought to live a life that I hoped would in some ways mimic the simplicity and independence of the people who also moved here for the same reasons some two-hundred-plus years ago, my own people included. My own family line left the southern Appalachians to find work in the late nineteenth century, but their ways remained, and perhaps this is what was lodged somewhere back in my genetic memory. I was a victim of my own romanticism in many ways, as it has never been the place of Foxfire, though the landscape and the spirit of this place still speak to me as powerfully as ever. I'm an outsider, though born just two hours away and with a southern pedigree that dates back to the early eighteenth century. My wife and I moved here imbued with what we thought was humility toward the people and the place but have learned from over two decades of living here that, with the exception of a minority of newcomers and open-minded locals, only the landscape, with its world-class biodiversity, spectacular beauty and cultural history, is worthy of it. And, of course, its connection to William Bartram.

Two years ago, at a celebration in Albuquerque honoring the fiftieth anniversary of this landmark legislation, I participated in a panel discussion on the Wilderness idea in American history. Bartram was my subject, and when I asked the group of fifty or so people if they had heard of William Bartram, only three or four raised their hands. However, when I asked how many people had seen or read the book *Cold Mountain* and remembered the strange book (*Travels*) that Inman kept close by and referred to as he made his way back home to the mountains, almost every hand in the room shot up. Inman quoted Bartram's descriptions of Appalachia because they are the most passionate renderings of their magnificence to this day. Plodding his way home, he describes the lowlands with disdain—the muddy rivers, bad roads, mean people—and Appalachia, much as it was to Bartram, and with his aid, is elevated to the sublime. I don't mean to imply that this feeling isn't shared by most locals and newcomers residing here today but only that this is no longer the landscape of Foxfire or any other number of publications exalting Appalachian culture, both real and imagined.

Aldo Leopold, famous for his shift in thinking after seeing the fierce green fire in the dying eyes of a wolf he had shot, said of the founding of the Wilderness Society in 1935 that the society is philosophically a disclaimer of the biotic arrogance of Homo americanus. It is one of the focal points of a new attitude—an intelligent humility toward man's place in nature. But humility is one emotion that is increasingly in short supply in the recently defined geological epoch, the Anthropocene, where we now dominate and control nature, and where Wilderness and past ideas of the wild are considered outdated, irrelevant and destined for the dustbin of history. Nature, once the romantic construct that grounded the conservation movement in both its science and emotion, is being deconstructed and reconstructed to define us in this new geological era as gardeners and ambitious utilitarians who must manage and restore, as we are now completely in control. Humans are the dominant species, and nature is ours completely. Humility is for losers.

For me, someone who is working to conserve our last wild places in the southern Appalachians, these ideas are making the effort increasingly challenging. Bartram's idea of Wilderness as sublime and the evolution of this idea into Wilderness legislated have already suffered the effects of academic deconstruction, but couple this with the dull ideology of the Anthropocene, along with the growing wave of those who want no limits when it comes to human activities, and advocacy for these ideas takes place in difficult terrain. Here in western North Carolina, where over one million acres of federal public lands make up almost a quarter of total ownership, a new management plan is being created that will determine their future for the next fifteen to twenty years. Wilderness is a piece of this, as new Wilderness areas can be recommended as part of this plan. With only about 6 percent of this current acreage designated as such, it seems reasonable that we would protect more, yet advocates seem less and less enthusiastic while opponents seem to grow in rancor and numbers. Humility and sublimity have no place at the planning table, for management advocates on all sides of the table want all land open always to whatever activities they see appropriate to meet human desires—whether it's restoration or the need to be able to access and manage for game species. Arguing with these values for the protection of nature at this table places one in a camp of outdated romantics, out of touch with Anthropocene reality and unwilling to move on.

So what does wild mean anymore, and why trouble myself with these heady thoughts of the sublime here in the cynical twenty-first century? Maybe if nostalgic views of wild nature are truly bound for the dustbin, where ideas and viewpoints sometimes rightfully go, I should just get over it. But if these ideas no longer have a place at the table within the modern-day discourse of the Anthropocene, what does this mean for art and poetry, both of which draw from the human constructs of beauty and enrich and humble us before nature? And what can the Anthropocene offer in return? Beauty in our engineering and technology, our final and ultimate conquest? Maybe we need this idea of the sublime more than ever as a species. It might help center us in our insignificance within the great scheme of biodiversity and evolution and humble us before all creation. And perhaps the ideas and appreciation of Wilderness and wild nature will continue to enrich our imaginations, should we decide to keep them, expanding our capacity to accept limits, grounding us in civilized restraint.

Every neotropical bird here has left or is preparing to leave, as it has since the Pleistocene epoch, a geological period that forced migrations of species southward during its ice age, much like this current geological Anthropocene era and its record heat is ironically forcing these same species farther north. Unfortunately, they will never engineer their way out of this mess. Audubon predicts that many of these species will vanish from the southern Appalachians, moving farther north or crashing altogether. Occasionally over the last few weeks, I've heard hooded warblers and black throated green warblers singing, a strange time of year for them to do this, but I expect they are the young of the year, practicing their newly acquired songs. It's magic to the ear if one is attuned so. It adds to the melancholy these mountains seem to propagate in the fall, when chill winds begin to blow and the light begins to shift in dramatic and ethereal brightness and shadow. They're likely gone now, winging their way south across the Caribbean to places like Colombia or Nicaragua. Habitat in these winter ranges is dwindling due to deforestation, and coupled with climate change, their situation is becoming all the more dire. I cannot imagine an Appalachian spring without them, just as I cannot imagine a world where this would be acceptable. Their arrival is that spectacular and uplifting, that sublime.

PUSHING THROUGH

2:30 a.m., Thicket Branch, Great Smoky Mountains National Park, late September 2017. I have been "walking" since 9:00 a.m., though walking is no way to describe the last ten hours. It has been crawling, pushing, climbing and scrambling through the densest rhododendron I have ever seen in my life. And I've seen a fair amount. Prior to that, I waded 3.4 miles up the east fork of Raven Fork, within one of the wildest pieces of country left in the eastern United States. It was a leisurely wade, fishing for native brook trout, through an old-growth red spruce forest where enormous hemlocks have succumbed to hemlock wooly adelgid, choking the stream at times and forcing us to perform the limbo and various acrobatic feats. We had no idea what to expect when we exited the stream at 4:30 p.m., thinking we would bushwhack our way up to the ridge line above us and walk the 3 miles back down to campsite 44, where we had backpacked to the previous afternoon.

Brook trout in this high-elevation stream appear as ghosts from the light of my headlamp, blue, translucent. Maybe they are. I could be hallucinating after so much exertion, and I still have no idea when we will make it back to camp, or if we will. I'm beyond fatigued and have been dehydrated for the last six hours. In my near delirium, I think of this as another metaphor for the last three months of my life. Today, we left our camp at McGee Spring and bushwhacked our way down to the east fork of Raven Fork, much as we did last year, though instead of heading downstream to Three Forks, where three streams form a great pool amidst high-elevation old-growth spruce forest, we head upstream, to country we have not ventured to before. It's a trip I've needed since losing my job in May, a job I believed would sustain me until retirement and a job I'd given my all to, with people I believed in. At fifty-eight, this is nothing to be taken lightly, and so heading into some of the most rugged terrain in the eastern United States was something I believed I needed to get grounded again after depression and outright despair.

A close friend and past hiking companion who is ninety-four calls me a few days before I leave and pleads with me not to go alone. He's a retired neurologist and knows me well. He's concerned about my depression and knows that people often come to this park to die, like wild sick animals leaving their kin to pass away quietly and without attention. I assure him I'm not that depressed and that I will contact a friend who I have hiked with many times before about joining me.

Campsite 44, McGee Springs. A high-elevation campsite amidst old-growth spruce-fir forest, at the dead end of the trail, with nothing but wildness before me. Here alone I sit, a box of wine and a journal, red breasted nuthatches and golden crowned kinglets singing in the spruce. A raven circles over twice, so close I can hear its wings flapping in the clear September sky. Happy, feeling lighter than I have in months, I write of what is around me and am grateful for the moment. My planned solo trip is now aborted as I wait for another close friend, Herman Walker, who has explored this part of the park with me before and knows the difficult terrain. He is likely beginning his hike up from Round Bottom Road as I write and will be here in a few hours. Drink this in, I think. Take it all in, as much as possible—the air, the smell of spruce, the wine, the insects I observe beneath my hand lens.

There is no trail up Raven Fork, only flowing water, boulders, logjams of dead hemlocks and spruce and dense and ever-present rhododendron flanking it all. We spend over seven hours traveling 3.4 miles up this holy and untouched place. This large area of the park was never logged due to its inaccessibility, and its magnificence is stupefying—Jurassic. I remark to Herman at one point that I expect to see dinosaurs or a bigfoot emerge at any moment. It seems that incongruous with the world I have just departed from.

For most of the day, we fish. Herman is either upstream or downstream from me, always within shouting distance, he with his dry flies and consistent enthusiasm for catching native brook trout and me alone with my constant ruminations and rage. The beauty of the place and the occasional brook trout I reel in soften the feelings, but the feelings are as present as always. I want to purge them and explode into this place—to be one with it and its power, which is beyond my comprehension. I've always felt outraged by injustice, but this is the first time in my life I have experienced it in such a direct and life-impacting situation. It never quite leaves my consciousness. I dream about it. Write in my journal about it. I wake in the middle of the night and think about it. And as much as I want to will a new life, and a new self, it refuses to leave. I know it will take time.

So all day now, while staring into the gin-clear water and exploring gravel bars, I have been thinking about how a major conservation organization that I had given over ten of the best years of my life to threw me under the bus because two rich funders wanted something I could not deliver on. I've dealt with rich funders all of my life, so that was nothing new. I'd just never seen how one individual could work so effectively to undermine the efforts of another solely because he had wealth. Not competence—wealth. This individual disagreed with the outcome of a collaborative effort that took over two years to negotiate, and for the next two years he worked to destroy it—and did. The organization I worked for had initially supported the effort and outcome and praised it nationally as a model. So did the forty-plus organizations that had been part of the process. But when this individual, who had never been part of the process, and who represented only himself, found about the process and outcome, he immediately went to the biggest conservation funder in North Carolina and convinced him that it was a bad outcome.

I shake my head a lot, my wife tells me, and I catch myself doing this as I wade upstream, thinking, thinking. At 4:30 p.m., we decide it is a wise time to stop and head back to camp. We clean a dozen brook trout, put them in a Ziploc with wet moss and look at the steep slope above us that we must climb to get to the summit of Hyatt Ridge. Neither of us having done this before, we assume it will be easier than wading the stream back to McGee Springs. We've made these types of journeys before, and though the forest above us appears dense with rhododendron, we aren't intimidated by it. We'll push through it to the ridge and stroll on back to camp. I take the fish, and we both decide that we don't need to purify more water, as we both have a little and consider it enough for the hike back, which we think we can do in two to three hours. Wading a mountain stream for seven hours is no easy task, and we are a bit tired and beat up but are in good spirits and condition to do this. We joke about the bourbon back at camp, wish we'd brought it and begin the climb.

After an hour, we've made little progress. The rhododendron is dense and snarled together, and we must crawl, climb and force our way through with great energy being expended. After three hours, we are becoming dehydrated and have not even gone a mile. It is getting dark, and I'm feeling a bit uneasy as I look at the GPS unit and see how much farther we have to go, with no sign of the rhododendron letting up. I drink the water out of a tuna package, eat my last two carrots and stare into the tangle. At 1:00 a.m. and having not yet made it a fourth of the way back to camp, we are both approaching exhaustion and feeling desperate for water. It is slowly sinking in that we are not going to make it back to camp this way tonight and that we have got to get to water. We find a blue line stream down the ridge on the iHike app that Herman has on his iPhone, and with his dying battery, we begin descending through snarls of rhododendron that are seemingly without end. At almost 2:00 a.m., we find the stream, and after filling ourselves and our bottles, I attempt to talk Herman into spending the night. We have matches, but there is little to burn but rhododendron, and besides, Herman is concerned that in our condition we are ripe for hypothermia and will find ourselves unable to go on if we rest.

I agree, somewhat reluctantly, as I fear that sooner or later one of us is going to take a bad fall. It is treacherous beyond belief, and as we peck our way down Thicket Branch, the stream grows, and we soon find ourselves delicately clamoring down waterfalls and over and under enormous downed spruce trees that span the stream. I am trying not to become angry. This was a trip that I had wanted for myself since losing my job in May. I wanted the park for solace, inspiration and self-renewal, and here I am now thinking that I could die. Irony begins to sink in, along with the liberating idea that all my anger and frustration over the past summer has been an illusion. I begin to think of other ironies.

My first trip into this park alone was the summer I turned eighteen. I had just graduated from high school, and I was largely friendless at the time. High school was not pleasant for me. In my senior year, my abusive stepfather became worse, drinking heavily and taking his frustrations out on me and anyone else he could lash out at in our household. I worked every day from 5:30 to 9:30 p.m. at United Parcel Service, loading and unloading trucks, and after work smoked weed and drank heavily to cope with it all. The stepfather left around the time of my graduation, but it was too late. I had withdrawn and found my only solace in the forest behind our house, the one that had saved me so many times before. While others in my graduating class went on celebratory cruises or drove to Daytona Beach for drunken revelry, I worked even more, planning my own getaway to backpack across the Smokies, following the Appalachian Trail to its starting point in Georgia.

I knew nothing of backpacking, only that I wanted the experience and was willing to try. My mother drove me to Cosby campground on the east end of the park and left me with inadequate gear and a mind full of darkness. I was caught in an August thunderstorm almost as soon as she left. It didn't end, and after a few hours of hiking through it wearing a cheap poncho and without a cover for my pack, I was completely soaked, as was all of my gear. With dark coming on, I realized that I had missed the trail that would take me to a point on the Appalachian Trail where my first backcountry reservation was made. I had no tent, only a small tarp, and I soon also realized that I would not make it to the shelter. I had gone miles out of my way, and there was no going forward. I slept wrapped in the tarp while the rain fell, tired but still full of determination to make my destination, almost two hundred miles away. The experience of surviving this night out alone, and the subsequent trail challenges, changed me. I came home more confident and more in love with wild places than ever before.

The irony that I am here in this park now forty years later, with much more experience, but in a somewhat similar situation, does not escape me. In my pack is an Eagle Claw fishing rod that accompanied me on that teenage trip and that I have treasured ever since, only using it for these deep excursions in the park. Much like that night, tonight I want to bed down in the dry woods and sleep a deep and fatigued sleep and hack our way out once daylight arrives. But we push on, falling often, carefully clamoring downstream toward the east fork of Raven Fork. Two years ago, Herman lost a brother to an avalanche in the Cascade Mountains, and though I say nothing, I can't help but think that this must be on his mind, pushing him onward toward his wife, children and grandchildren. It is certainly pushing me onward. I'm also aware that a few people out there are worried about me. I reflect on the conversation I had with Bob before leaving, worrying now that the friend he wanted me to go with and I might die or become seriously injured in one of the most rugged places in the eastern United States. I can't help but think about my original intent to come here alone to sit among the old-growth spruce with a journal and pen and some small volumes of poetry and decompress—not to push myself harder physically and mentally than I ever have in my life.

Unless I am hallucinating, I am looking at what might be a national champion red spruce. What a gift, to experience wonder in the midst of mild terror. And the brook trout, small, blue and seemingly translucent in the weakening halogen headlamp. How did it all come to this? I stagger on. At a certain point in my self-loathing for getting myself into this, I attempt to shift my perspective. Maybe this is exactly what I need—pushing myself through this hell of rhododendron as a metaphor for a personal catharsis, this falling and stumbling and crawling my way through this dark night toward dawn and comfort, far off at the moment but not impossible.

We reach the east fork of Raven Fork at almost 4:00 a.m. and rest on a gravel bar where Thicket Branch enters the river. We pump more water and both remark upon our states of dehydration, which we attribute to adrenaline. This is the part of our journey I have feared the most. Difficult by day, I can't imagine what it will be like in darkness, as our headlamps fade, and we along with them after twelve hours of bushwhacking from our departure not far upstream from where we are now. With the GPS unit now dead, we must pay careful attention for the point where McGee Spring enters the east fork, as this is our only known route back to Hyatt Ridge and camp. If we miss it, we will no doubt spend the remainder of this night somewhere down in this gorge and will have to wait until daylight. We remember a flat spot on the west side of the river that was not far from the spring, and once we see it, we begin scanning the bank on the east, hugging it close and looking for a small piece of orange flagging that we had found earlier that day. I find it, and the spring, soon after, and though utterly exhausted, I feel as if I could spring up the steep and muddy mountainside for the half mile we must cover to make it back to camp.

When we arrive at camp at 5:30 a.m., I am so tired that I am disoriented and wander about, uncertain as to where the tents are, and consider that I am possibly lost somewhere in the upper reaches of McGee Spring. I find my tent at last, collapse inside and wake five hours later and check my body for damage. I'm still exhausted and have to hike four more miles out with a heavy pack. I decide to get up now and go for it while the adrenaline is still pumping. I have a half pint of Jack Daniels, and after packing and a quick breakfast, I put it in my pocket and begin the walk. Herman is awake, and we share a cup of coffee as he packs up. He is in good spirits, despite the obvious fatigue and exhaustion, and, for almost seventy, amazingly mobile and unfazed. I leave him packing and start the slow trudge toward the trailhead. I'm glad to be alone, sipping whiskey and confident about getting out and home. I don't even know what condition I'm in—I'm that tired—but I'm going home. Home to Epsom salts and deep sleep and a step further toward release from the self-inflicted torture I've imposed upon myself for months.

After recovering for a couple of days, I e-mail a good friend who documents champion trees and tell him about the spruce in Thicket

Branch. He immediately tells me that old-growth sleuth Will Blozan documented the national champion red spruce there several years ago, but no one had ever been able to verify it. This doesn't surprise me. Then I break out in a horrific rash. Every scrape and cut on my body, and there are many, becomes irritated with something that looks like poison ivy, though that isn't what it is. But what is it? My scientific explanation, based on Internet research, is that I am toxified by exposure to rhododendron. My pharmacist tells me it is not poison ivy, and Herman, who is allergic, says that he has not broken out. Besides, he says, we never saw poison ivy. It's rarely present in rhododendron. I consider it another metaphor with literal expression—I'm releasing all the emotional poison I have built up in me from the last five months. Do we really repeat our pasts throughout life, and are we structured psychologically to do so until we learn and move on? I'm no good at this. I have no life experience to call upon to point me in another direction. I've dealt with divorce, a bipolar child who suffered through years of addiction, work challenges of every sort, a difficult and traumatic childhood, but I've never had to call upon myself to rise again like I am now.

Within a week after I return, a package in the mail arrives from a friend. In it are copies of Pema Chödrön's *When Things Fall Apart* and Paul Kingsnorth's *Confessions of a Recovering Environmentalist*. I am familiar with Kingsnorth's work and have been reading his essays and novels for several years. He's a critic of the environmental movement and its obsession with "sustainability." The sustainability argument is closely linked to those advocates of the Anthropocene and its emphasis on our ability as humans to think our way out of the mess we're in. We're on top, the argument goes, and smart enough to figure things out with the natural world. We can control it, bend it to our will and, perhaps most importantly, fix it. Fix it with our technology and human wherewithal. Kingsnorth puts his bets on the Nature Bats Last philosophy, and I'm with him. Central to his message is letting go of hope in these dark times. Retreat and immerse yourself into the ecological grief of our era and find the art and creativity that is necessary to respond—engaged withdrawal.

Kingsnorth's message is for the individual seeking a way to cope with what is happening on a global scale today, but Chödrön's message is for the individual caught in his or her own web of personal despair and hopelessness. I'm seeking escape from my own anger and desires, caught up in my hurt ego and longing for revenge. Her message hits me hard. To think that we can finally get it all together is unrealistic. To seek for some lasting security is futile. Believing in a solid, separate self, continuing to seek pleasure and avoid pain, thinking that someone "out there" is to blame for our pain—one has to get totally fed up with these ways of thinking. Hopelessness means that we no longer have the spirit for holding our trip together. It's all suffering, it's all despair, and the sooner I can accept this the more beautiful and sadder it all becomes. I know I have to let go, that I can't keep going on at this age with such feelings of rage and emptiness. I love the world and the temporality of it all. And despite my long visit to the dark side, I see the light. I can emerge and find a new path. The world has always been this way.

WHICH WAY IS THE WILDERNESS?

Anyone who's made it into adulthood knows how quickly things can fall apart. One day you're fine, the next day you're punched in the gut and lying on the floor. In May 2017, I lost my job as a regional director with the Wilderness Society, and the loss was underhanded, full of betrayal and hidden agendas. At almost fifty-nine years of age, this was no minor bump in the road. I didn't know how to stand up. Over twenty-five years working in conservation, and now I was utterly disillusioned. Literally sickened by the circumstances. And with a paltry severance package, bills to pay and retirement still a long way off, I had no choice but to start seeking some type of immediate income. What I needed, though, had nothing to do with money—what I needed was to get as far away from my home in these North Carolina mountains as I could. Everywhere I turned here were reminders—people, places, memories and the forests I had loved and worked to protect for so long. So, in December 2017, I boarded a plane with my wife and left for a two-month trip to England, where several good friends who lived there were more than willing to help me sort out this new life.

England was to be a re-setting of the dial, though I realized there was no coming back from something like the life event I had gone through. Two wealthy individuals (heirs to fortune, I might add) did not like the result of a collaborative process I had led for four years, one which they had never participated in, and began a private campaign to discredit it. Why participate in such a process when you can simply use your influence to get the result you want? The pair had made my life miserable for two of the last four years, as they could get an immediate audience with the president of the organization I worked for, and being from a family fortune himself, he easily sided with these two. When he made the decision to support their opinion, I was given an option to support it or leave. Fifty-eight, no job. Go to England, be among friends, take long walks in the frozen moors and come back (or not) different.

Angela and I planned for months. I worked more than ever during this time but still had to withdraw from my retirement account to pay the bills and build our struggling new eco-tourism business. I led canoe trips and workshops, landed a couple of freelance writing gigs and worked as a landscaper. We sold a car. We sold personal possessions on eBay. We practiced letting go. December at last arrived, and we were suddenly airborne, the vortex of the last six months' uncertainties and fears subsiding with the long Atlantic crossing, each glass of wine on the plane washing it all down.

I was in England to build scar tissue and did. Late wintry afternoons in the pubs, epic road and train trips to Liverpool, Whitby, Berwick-upon-Tweed, Carlyle, Grasmere, London, wherever we were moved to go and whenever we felt like going. We spent a month in a Harrogate flat due to the generosity of our friends Alex Crowton and Sally Robertshaw and fell deep into the Christmas spirit of the place, taking road trips with them and their two lovely daughters, Willa and Betty, across England's north country. Christmas Day was a traditional holiday feast with their extended family in Grassington; Christmas night was spent shooting pool with all of them at the well-loved nearby pub, the Forester's Arms.

In January, we moved to a rented cottage as far out in the Yorkshire Dales as we could imagine: Middlesmoor, head of the Nidd River valley, with its one pub, the Crown, and its forty or so inhabitants who lived there full time. The last village at the end of the road from Pately Bridge, where every direction from our cottage offered long walks through the wild and empty moors. It must have seemed crazy to friends and family at home—us taking off in the middle of winter to live in another country, a cold and damp one at that, just because I couldn't somehow shake off the trauma of betrayal and job loss. But I was crazy, and crazy said get away, and as far away as I could. It didn't matter that financially I shouldn't do it. Or that a more "responsible" person would dust off that résumé, suck it up and go out and bang their head against that great American wall again looking for work.

Upon arrival in England, I let go of such notions. I flushed my anti-depressants, started to wean myself off Ambien and began writing poetry again. At Waterstone's in Harrogate, I loaded up on British nature

The author's cottage in Middlesmoor, England. *Photo by Brent Martin.*

writing, amazed at the sheer quantity of it and that, as a genre, it seemed to be enjoying a renaissance. However, one work stood out among the others and seemed apropos to our two-month stay in the north country: William Atkins's *The Moor: A Journey into English Wildness*. There was a certain intimacy in its connection to the landscape, an intimacy that I felt was somehow lacking in America, where the Anthropocene idea and its academic debates on wildness and Wilderness were driving one of many wedges into the conservation "movement."

I wished to forget this world of academic debates and return to the world of nature writers and artists—two groups that had led me to conservation work to begin with, ones that I had designated early on as creators and keepers of the flame. Our eighteenth-century cottage was loaded with local histories and maps, and I couldn't have been happier. Just outside the door to our cottage was the fifty-four-mile-long Nidderdale Way. I pored over Ordinance Survey map 298 and scribbled down the place names that surrounded us—Fountains Earth Moor, High Sikes, Blayshaw Crags, Shake Hole, Black Gutter Head, Flaytones, Ramsgill Bent, Cold Stone Cuts—

words that held mystery, storied and alive. It reminded me of the Cherokee place names that still existed in my home landscape. For the last several years, I had led courses on landscape and literature, and these courses were the products of place-based writing in the western North Carolina mountains. I always began with Robert Macfarlane's *Landmarks* and Barry Lopez's *Home Ground: Language for an American Landscape* for introductions on how language connects us to our geography and how imbedded it is in the history of locale. People seem to be hungry for these types of connections.

Looking back, I realize that these courses, which were taught during my vacation time while working in conservation, were ways of keeping me sane in a job that seemed to be driven by protecting place but that politics and controversial attitudes on "management" had stripped of inherent sacredness and respect. It was all about us—humans—and what we wanted and needed, with an utter absence of humility. In a multi-year public planning process for over one million acres of national forest land where I live, those such as myself who wanted to see more of the land permanently protected and withdrawn from management were

The Nidderdale Way, Middlesmoor, England. *Photo by Brent Martin.*

increasingly marginalized and put on the defense. It's not all that different than the re-wilding movement in England, where opposition is largely rural and fear based, though in America it is inverse, as the controversy seems to focus on taking our last wild areas and opening them up for resource extraction or intensive management for more game species.

The moors stretched for miles in every direction, and it mattered little to me as to their naturalness. The land had been worked and cleared for so many millennia that wildness and Wilderness seemed relative, and regardless, there were wide-open spaces to wander in, and all I wanted to do was wander. William Atkins addresses this eloquently in *The Moor*: "The moors could be wild, but wilderness? It was no more than an idea." According to the deconstructionists, it's always been an idea, but so what. What isn't? It's an argument I've heard against Wilderness for a long, long time: western civilization invented our romanticized version of Wilderness following our conquest of the New World. Wilderness before and during settlement: bad; Wilderness following settlement and conquest: good. Native Americans on my continent had no word for it. Settlers displaced them from their native homes and then sanitized their landscape of them and all things wild that threatened their objectives, then romanticized the landscape to their liking. Opponents of all stripes to the modern Wilderness idea delegitimize it with this history; Anthropocene advocates argue that regardless of this deconstruction, it all needs human hands to keep it healthy and serving us.

To Atkins, hikers coming to the North Pennines not far from our cottage to experience "England's Last Wilderness" could care less about true Wilderness anyway, however you'd like to define it. As he says, it's no more than a slogan. What I identify with is his idea that hikers want something darker. It was not just "Wilderness" that brought those lone hikers to the causey paving, not even a mistaken or deluded notion of "Wilderness"; it was something darker: "a desire to experience ruination and expose oneself in the aftermath of catastrophe." It's an interesting idea. Much like designated Wilderness areas near my home in the southern Appalachians, the moors have all been altered and disturbed previously by humans. People coming to visit Shining Rock Wilderness area in western North Carolina are told at interpretive kiosks that the vast open balds are the result of massive industrial logging and subsequent wildfires. It's one of the most visited Wilderness areas in the eastern United States. Atkins's once forested and now highly altered moors are no different. What matters is that these areas feel wild to such seekers, and their history of disturbance and inherent ability to return to whatever

The Pennine Way, Malham Cove, England. *Photo by Brent Martin.*

perhaps makes them all the wilder. Here in Middlesmoor, with How Stean Beck carving its way through the upper Nidd valley in a deep limestone gorge lined with caves and ancient English oaks, and red grouse exploding from the gorse as we walked the Nidderdale Way to the abandoned village of Scar House Moss, I felt wild for the first time in a long while too.

During my last week in England, my wife and I travel to London so that I can meet a much-anticipated appointment with the William Bartram collection at the library of the Natural History Museum. The appointment has been arranged months in advance, and it is a collection I have wanted access to for many years. When I reach the inner sanctum of the library, the generous and helpful staff point toward a large cart where the eighteenth-century American naturalist's artwork is housed in several large boxes. It had belonged to John Fothergill, an English doctor and primary patron of Bartram, and knowing that I have only six hours, I am immediately overwhelmed. I follow the well-established protocols and place the first painting on a display table. A curlew on a beach with an urchin, exquisite and fine in its attention and detail. I scratch a few notes down and proceed

Howstean Beck, Middlesmoor, England. *Photo by Brent Martin.*

through a dazzling display of early American natural history—alligators, snakes, birds, plants, landscapes—until at last I reach the final box. I had wondered all day when I would encounter his famous painting of the now extinct *Franklinia*, found once in the wild and existing today only because

William Bartram's *Franklinia alatamaha* at Natural History Museum, London. *Photo by Brent Martin.*

of his propagation. It's the end of the day, and I spend a long while with it before returning it to its home.

Bartram is credited with being the first American to use the term *Wilderness* in a romantic fashion, describing my southern home landscape with rhapsodic language, and—counter to the American attitude of the time—portraying sympathy, humility and respect toward the region's Native Americans. Contrary to prevailing attitudes of the time, Bartram was elevating wildness to the sublime, and he not only exported his plants and art to England, he exported the Wilderness idea through his 1791 publication, *Travels*. *Travels* is an odd amalgamation of scientific observation and effusive romantic ramblings, a first of its kind and the beginning of American natural history. Though received lukewarmly in America, mainly due to its sympathetic treatment of Native Americans, it was warmly received and borrowed from in England by Wordsworth and Coleridge, its influence making its way back to America a few decades later to Thoreau and Emerson. This was the end of the Enlightenment, when man stood at the top of the Great Chain of Being, his faculties superior over all other living creatures, imbued with the creator's gift of reason and law. Emotional truth, and the gift of the senses, gained ground and began its course alongside and in competition with science, an intellectual divide that has continued to its zenith today in western civilization. Today, advocates for the romantic ideas of Wilderness and wildness on both sides of the Atlantic clamor to be heard over the advocates of the new era of the Great Chain of Being, the Anthropocene.

Regardless, Bartram's romantic 1775 descriptions of my home landscape are what hold me to it, just as history and mythologies around the moors hold its inhabitants and visitors to it. It's where I've settled in intellectually when thinking about how we connect to place and where we are headed as a species. I can see what we've done to my homeplace geography 223 years later, and I don't trust ideas of human superiority and their ability to save the planet. It's what gave us atomic bombs, unsustainable agriculture, a dysfunctional political system, industrial manufacturing, global pollution and imperialism, to name but a few. I'd rather put my faith in humility and respect for what's left of the wild and natural world.

Home. I don't really want to return to it, though I miss my own *Franklinia* and our little mountain farm it grows on. And as much as I have fallen in love with the wild and empty moors, I do miss the rich, dense forests of the Appalachians. Before leaving England, we go with friends to see the movie *Three Billboards Outside Ebbing, Missouri*. It was filmed in Sylva, North Carolina, not far from our home, and seeing the Balsam Mountains for the first time in almost two months makes my heart roar and the tears rise. And though it is set in a midwestern state, the movie's violence and characters are southern in nature and humor, and whether I like it or not, those are my people. I have to go home.

THE NEW INGLES GROCERY store near downtown Franklin, North Carolina, is the largest store I've been in for over two months. It may be the largest store I've been in anywhere, ever. I'm looking for the section where I can buy soap, which it seems should be self-evident, but the section where it should be is vast, full of health and beauty products, supplements, shampoos and conditioners, and when I do at last find it, it's daunting. The section is about the size of the entire grocery store where my family shopped when I was a child. I haven't slept much the last two nights, and yesterday was one of the worst travel experiences I've ever had. A delayed flight out of London, a missed flight in Toronto, a later flight that was also delayed, a lost boarding pass, singled out in security and having to remove every item in my carry-on for inspection, etc. But we need groceries, and here I am, staring at the small print on soap packaging looking for something without palm oil. All I want is to get in and out of this enormous monstrosity without seeing anyone I know. I'm not ready to see anyone here in Franklin, having been gone two months and having left because I needed a break from this place and a ten-year run of difficulties. Soap. How could it become so damned complicated? We never had to think about palm oil until now, what with the Internet and its ghastly images of clear-cut forests and endangered birds. I might fall asleep standing right here staring at the soap section.

"Hey, which way is the Wilderness?" a voice proclaims from somewhere behind me. Am I dreaming? An auditory hallucination? I wonder. I hope so. I turn, and standing before me is the local district ranger for the U.S. Forest Service. He smiles and says something else that doesn't register, but I try to laugh and make small talk. It's impossible. He's the last person I want to see today, and if he knew how rhetorical and empty the question sounded to me, he might not have asked it. No, he would have. Then again, I think I needed to hear it, and from him on this first day back.

I could have pointed toward the rear of the store and said, "That way," the Southern Nantahala Wilderness being less than ten miles in that direction, or toward the store entrance, with Ellicott Rock Wilderness being about the same. Or I could have pointed toward my or his chest, straight toward our hearts. Or toward the sky. I could have shaken my head as I am shaking it now, remorseful at the question, wondering how I ever became the person who would be asked it here at the burnt-out end of a Wilderness-saturated career. Instead, I attempt to laugh it off. But it feels ugly, and I want to get on the next flight back to England. There is something powerfully serendipitous about this encounter. *Welcome home*, says the universe, *here's a complimentary koan for you. Stop thinking about it, and buy some soap*, I respond. He leaves, and I continue with my struggle. After a bleary weak-eyed scan of ingredients, I settle on Kirk's Castille coconut oil soap, with its bright white and blue wrapper, sans palm oil, and hope it will be the one to satisfy the exacting demands of my wife's obsessive soap standards. Three bars, wrapped together, so simple and with such clear purpose and future. To clean! To clean. To be washed down a drain, the remains to settle in our decrepit septic tank. Oh, to have such clarity of purpose.

There is a brand of soap called Wilderness, and it serves as a metaphor. If you look at the company online, it has a large assortment of scents and options, much like actual Wilderness and ideas of wildness. They're not cheap, and they would appeal to someone with disposable income or exacting soap standards. They also make me think of another metaphor—that these bars of soap are ideas that are washing the world clean of Wilderness. Ideas are cheap and seem to be getting cheaper, as anyone can come up with them and distribute them to a global audience. Wildness, though, we feel in our bones, whether we're scared shitless on a cold winter night when the car's broken down on a lonely mountain road, screaming down a crazy path on a mountain bike or sitting with a friend by a beautiful, pristine brook. It's not an idea; it's an experience. The wild world might howl in whispers these days, but it's there, whether we attune to it, ignore it or engage in academic debates about it. It could care less what brand of soap I buy or if I've lost a job trying to protect it. Or at least that's how I like to think about it.

Which way is the Wilderness? Every way. As many ways as can be imagined. I do want to walk out of this Ingles with my three bars of soap and find some solace from the question, but I'm not sure if I will. I've asked it a long time, and at this age, maybe I've been asking it the wrong way. Home is a place where Cherokee words still define the landscape. Cartoogechaye. Cowee. Nantahala. Kituwah. Cullasaja. They had no word for Wilderness and did not seek it. I want to be able to answer it, for it feels relevant in a world diminishing of wildness, where the question itself might have a short life span. I do feel to point inward to an answer could also be to point outward. It could be that.

INDEX

A

Abbey, Edward 29
Adair, James 57
  History of the American Indians 57
Afro-Caribbean 83
Alabama 44, 50, 51
Alarka Laurel 24
Alexander, Ted 99, 100
  Mountain Fever 99
Altamaha River 48, 57
American Revolution 17, 20, 71, 108
Anthropocene 38, 113, 114, 123
Aphrodite 86
Appalachia 20, 43, 47, 53, 99,
      112, 113
Appalachians 21, 45, 53, 55, 102,
      112, 113, 114
Appalachian Trail 120
Atakullahkullah 20

Atkins, William
  *The Moor: A Journey into English
      Wildness* 127, 129
Audubon 79, 114

B

Bartram, John 67
Bartram's Garden 67, 68, 72
Bartram Trail 80
Bartram Village 67
Bartram, William 15, 18, 19, 20, 21,
      22, 24, 26, 34, 45, 47, 48, 50, 57,
      64, 67, 68, 70, 72, 73, 108, 109,
      110, 112, 113, 130, 132, 133
  Travels 15, 18, 19, 22, 45, 68, 72,
      108, 110, 113, 132
Belt, Thom 109
Bemis Lumber 31
Beowulf 34

Big Snowbird 29, 30, 31, 36
Big Snowbird Creek 29, 30, 31, 41
Black's Creek 60, 61
Blozan, Will 123
Blue Ridge Mountains 18, 55, 56,
      57, 61, 63
Botany of Desire 50
Bribri Indian 83
brook trout 102
Burke, Sir Edmund 107

C

camellias 43, 46
Cameron, Alexander 21
Center for Spiritual Awareness 46
Charleston, South Carolina 19, 47, 70
Cherohala Skyway 29
Cherokees 15, 17, 18, 19, 20, 22,
      24, 25, 27, 33, 39, 43, 55, 56,
      57, 58, 60, 61, 62, 64, 70, 71,
      72, 73, 79, 90, 96, 103, 104,
      105, 108, 109
Cherokee villages
  Cowee, Nikwasee, Watauga,
      Keowee, Tellico, Overhill
      Towns 19, 73, 96
Chödrön, Pema 123
Chungke 62
Civil War 17
Cold Mountain 113
colonial trading paths 47
Costa Rica 83
Cowee 15, 17, 18, 19, 20, 21, 22,
      24, 25, 26, 27, 55, 70, 72, 73,
      75, 84, 87, 92, 95, 97, 107,
      108, 109, 112
Cowee Mountains 24, 45, 72, 73, 96
Cowee National Historic District 24
coyotes 33, 36, 41

Cullasaja 24
Cumberland Plateau 44

D

Darling Spring 59, 60, 61
Davis, Roy 46
Deliverance 39
Dickey, James
    Deliverance 57
Dickinson, Emily 20
Druids 92

E

Eastern Continental Divide 56
Edwards, Lawrence 95
Emanuel African Methodist
        Episcopal Church 70
Emerson, Ralph Waldo 112
ethnobotanical 24, 108

F

federal public lands 114
Fed Raby poplar 95
Flower Seeker, the 19
Fort Barrington 48
Fothergill, John 108, 130
Foxfire 112, 113
Franklinia 50, 93, 131, 133
Franklinia alatamaha 48, 68
Franklin, North Carolina 19, 133
Frasier magnolia 51
Frazer, Sir James
    Golden Bough, The 92
French and Indian War 17, 19, 20,
      62, 70
Fugitive, The 36

G

Galphin, George 21
Georgia 29, 43, 44, 48, 51, 56, 57, 68, 85, 94, 120
Gouge, Avery 102
Graham County 30, 33, 35, 39, 40
Great Smoky Mountains National Park 18, 30, 43, 99, 101, 102, 117
Guyot, Arnold 100

H

Harper's 18, 62
Hatley, Tom 58
   Dividing Paths 58
Hera 86
Herbert, John 57
Herbert's Savannah 57
Herbert's Spring 57, 60, 62, 63
Hicks, Phillip Marshall
   Development of the Natural History Essay in American Literature, The 110
honey locusts 22
Hooper Bald 29, 30
Horseshoe Bend 43, 46, 54
Huckleberry Branch 24
Humboldt Current 77
Humboldt penguins 77, 78
Hyatt Ridge 99, 119, 122

I

Islas Ballestas 75, 80

J

Jenkins, Peter
   Walk Across America, A 35, 39

Johnston, Jack 43
Joyce Kilmer–Slickrock Wilderness 30
Jupiter 92

K

Kautz, Jim
   In the Footsteps of William Bartram 22
Kephart, Horace 102
King Manu 86
Kingsnorth, Paul
   Confessions of a Recovering Environmentalist 123
Kostoyeak 61

L

Lake Allatoona 85
Lake Fontana 26
Lanman, Charles
   Letters from the Allegheny Mountains 61
Laurens, Henry 20
Leopold, Aldo 35, 113
Little Tennessee River 18, 19, 24, 25, 26, 43, 44, 57, 60, 84, 97
Little Tennessee River Valley 18, 66, 71
London 126, 130, 134
Lopez, Barry 73, 128
Lyon, John 48

M

Macfarlane, Robert 128
Mante, Thomas 57
Mars 95
Marshall, Lamar 19, 25, 58, 103
Masa, George 100, 102
maypops 24

McGee Springs (Breakneck Ridge) 100, 104, 105, 118

McLachlan, Carrie 58

Mclarney, William 25

Middlesmoor 126, 130

Middle Town 71, 108

Mighty Writers 71

Milarch, Dave

  Man Who Planted Trees, The 95

mistletoe 92

Mitchell Lick Trail 30

Moon, Beth 97

Mooney, James 27, 55, 57

Moonshiners 36, 39

Moore, George 29

mountain camellia 43, 47, 48, 50, 94

Mountain City, Georgia 19

Murfree, Mary Noailles (Charles Egbert Craddock)

  Harper's 61

Murphy 103

N

Nantahala Mountains 18, 20, 22, 45, 55, 72, 108

Nantahala River 20

Nash, Roderick 33, 108

  Wilderness and the American Mind 108

national champion red spruce 121, 123

Native American 16, 22, 58, 110

Nell 35

New World 43

Nidd River 126

Nikwasee 19, 72

North Carolina 24, 27, 30, 33, 35, 40, 43, 44, 45, 47, 51, 68, 70, 75, 79, 80, 84, 95, 96, 100, 108, 110, 114, 119

northern red oak 89, 90

North Pennines 129

O

Oconee County, South Carolina 48

Old Testament 80

Overhill Towns 18, 20, 22, 26

P

Paracas 75, 78

Pately Bridge 126

Peru 75, 77, 80, 81

Philadelphia 67, 68, 71, 72

Polk County, North Carolina 95

Pollan, Michael 50

Puerto Viejo (Gondoca Forest Reserve, Cahuita National Park) 83

Puritans 34

R

Rabun County, Georgia 43, 45

Raven Fork 99, 100, 101, 102, 104, 117, 118, 121, 122

Ravensford 100, 101

red legged cormorants 77

Red Spruce 24

Rilke, Rainer Maria 89, 93

river cane (*Arundinaria gigantea*) 24

Romantic movement (Wordsworth, Emerson, Coleridge, Thoreau) 34, 108, 110, 112

Roof, Dylann 70

Rudolph, Eric 33, 103

Rutherford, Griffith 71

S

Sanders, Brad 19, 21
Saturnalia 93
Sawmill Creek 51
Seminoles 19
Shabbat 80
Slaughter, Thomas P.
   Natures of John and William Bartram,
      The 20
Snowbird Mountains 29
Snowbird Wilderness Study Area 29
South Carolina 19, 58, 70
Sri Yukteswar 52
State Natural Heritage Program 97
Stecoah 35
Stewartia 48
Stewartia malacodendron (silky
      camellia) 48, 50
Stewartia ovata. See mountain
      camellia
sublime
   idea of 34, 45, 93, 107, 108, 113,
      114, 115
Sylva, North Carolina 133

T

Tennvannah 60, 61, 63
Theaceae 50
Thoreau, Henry David 110
Three Billboards Outside Ebbing,
      Missouri 133
Three Forks 99, 100, 101, 102,
      103, 104, 105, 106, 117
Tsali 33
Typhon 86

U

Unaka 18
U.S. Forest Service 17, 134

V

Viracocha 76, 80
Vishnu 86

W

Walker, Herman 118
Watauga 72, 73, 109
Watauga Town 72
Waynesville 36
Western Carolina University 58
white oaks (*Quercus alba*) 96
Wilderness 30, 33, 35, 37, 38, 39,
      113, 125, 129, 134, 135
Wilderness Act 35, 37
Wilderness and the American Mind 33
Wilderness Society, the 30, 113
Williams, Philip Lee 19
Williams, Terry Tempest 80
Wohlleben, Peter
   Hidden Life of Trees, The 93
Woodard, Honor 62
Wood, John 97

Y

Yamasee 61
yaupon holly (*Ilex vomitoria*) 24
Yogananda 46
Yucca filamentosa 24

Z

Zeus 92

ABOUT THE AUTHOR

Brent Martin is the author of three chapbook collections of poetry, *Poems from Snow Hill Road* (New Native Press, 2007), *A Shout in the Woods* (Flutter Press, 2010) and *Staring the Red Earth Down* (Red Bird Chapbooks, 2014), and is a coauthor of *Every Breath Sings Mountains* (Voices from the American Land, 2011) with authors Barbara Duncan and Thomas Rain Crowe. He is also the author of *Hunting for Camellias at Horseshoe Bend*, a nonfiction chapbook published by Red Bird Chapbooks in 2015. His poetry and essays have been published in the *North Carolina Literary Review*, *Pisgah Review*, *Tar River Poetry*, *Chattahoochee Review*, *Eno Journal*, *New Southerner*, *Kudzu Literary Journal*, *Smoky Mountain News* and elsewhere. He lives in the Cowee community in western North Carolina, where he and his wife, Angela Faye Martin, run Alarka Institute, a nature, literary and art-based business that offers workshops and field trips. He has recently completed a two-year term as Gilbert-Chappell Distinguished Poet for the West.

Visit us at
www.historypress.com
....